She's A
HOST

She's A HOST

An Unbuttoned Cookbook for
Elegant Entertaining

Erin Dana Lichy

Publisher Mike Sanders
Art & Design Director William Thomas
Editorial Director Ann Barton
Senior Editor Molly Ahuja
Designer Laura Palese
Photographer Linda Xiao
Food Stylist Monica Pierini
Prop Stylist Julia Rose
Recipe Tester Melissa Schwimmer
Copyeditor Mira S. Park
Proofreader Claire Safran
Indexer Beverlee Day

First American Edition, 2025
Published in the United States by DK Publishing
1745 Broadway, 20th Floor, New York, NY 10019

The authorized representative in the EEA is Dorling Kindersley Verlag
GmbH. Arnulfstr. 124, 80636 Munich, Germany

A catalog record for this book
is available from the Library of Congress.
ISBN 978-0-5939-7090-4

DK books are available at special discounts when purchased
in bulk for sales promotions, premiums, fund-raising, or educational use.
For details, contact SpecialSales@dk.com

Printed and bound in China

www.dk.com

This book is dedicated to my dad, Eli Yitzhari, who taught me that without love, nothing is worth living for.

CONTENTS

Welcome!

I'm delighted to share my most treasured recipes with you, along with the no-hassle, casually elegant approach to entertaining I use to celebrate life with my family and friends.

Welcoming people to the table has been a part of my life for as long as I can remember. When I was young, we had a Shabbat tradition: Dad kept the front door unlocked so anyone who needed a meal and some company could drop in for dinner. That's still the heart and soul of how I cook and entertain (thanks, Dad!). There is always room for one more at our table, and always enough food to fill another plate.

That idea is what makes this so much more than a cookbook. Honestly? It's a love letter. It's a tribute to uniquely heartfelt meals that bring people together and make life richer and more enjoyable. I wrote it to help you level up your own gatherings and make them all occasions like my family's Shabbat dinners—moments to share, cherish, and remember.

My relationship with food and community was entirely shaped by how I grew up. I'm the daughter and granddaughter of immigrants. My husband, too. Our family trees grow from roots spread throughout the Middle East, (including Iraq, Yemen, Israel, Turkey, and Greece) and south to Cuba. We're families of travelers and our journeys have always been as much about food as destination. I've enjoyed tantalizing shakshuka with a rowdy pack of cousins in Tel Aviv. I've indulged in perfectly ripe watermelon paired with subtly salty feta, under a blazing sun on a Mediterranean beach.

All that makes me feel so incredibly lucky. My heritage is a multicultural melting pot that comes to life in every dish I serve to friends and family. I learned from a young age that the meals we make are meant for a crowded table. It's the reason my recipes are the heart and soul of the entertaining I do. It's also why I'm so happy to share them with you.

My maternal grandmother helped me understand that food nourishes the soul as well as the body. Growing up in New York City, I spent tons of time with her. My mom was busy pioneering the real estate market around Lincoln Center, an area that had just begun to pop off (some may have called it up-and-coming). While she showed luxe apartments (and fostered my love of architecture and design—thanks, Mom!) to the likes of Brad and Gwyneth, I hung out with my grandma learning how to make the best food in the world.

She taught me that anything you cook and eat should be healthy, vibrant, comforting, and amazingly delicious. My happiest childhood memories are seasoned with the intoxicating smell of cumin and baharat wafting out of her oven. Even now, I can clearly see her strong, sinewy hands kneading huge balls of dough as she entertains me with amazing stories from her past.

My father's mother was just as strong an influence. On our frequent visits to Israel, she showed me that even the best food tasted better when shared. The entire Yemenite Dahari clan was clustered in a three-block radius in the center of Ramat Gan. Each family member had their mouthwatering specialty. Aunt Tzipi made to-die-for spicy Moroccan fish (page 157). My grandma served Yemenite soup (page 128) that still makes me hungry every time I think about it. Aunt Mali created scrumptious desserts that were the absolute perfect ending to any meal. Every dish was an open-door social occasion, and you never knew who would show up. It was like our own personal food court.

No surprise that I'm following in the footsteps of those strong, talented women . . . in my own way. I'm a busy wife and mom with four kids, businesses to run, and a TV show to film. Everything I cook has to fit into a crazy-packed schedule, but I'm not about to compromise. I would be too ashamed of what my grandmothers would have thought.

And I'm doing everything I can to pass the traditions on. It's no fluke that after his first day of school, my oldest son came sniffing through the cracked door and said, *"Are you making Yemenite soup? That's my favorite!"* The kids all dropped their backpacks and crowded into the kitchen to help me prep the meal. They may love boxed mac and cheese (who doesn't?), but their hearts beat faster at the smell of Za'atar Meatballs (page 161) or Picadillo (page 137). Dinners with them are my happiest times and remind me of what's most important in life.

That's what it's really all about, isn't it? Gathering with family and friends to break bread together. Being spontaneous, effortless, and joyful. It's the opposite of fussing or trying to be perfect. My kids have taught me that perfection is unrealistic. Instead, relax. Raise a glass. Celebrate life, because there is so much to celebrate. I wrote this book to help you do that. So, always remember: the most important ingredient is love. Well, and salt!

XO,

Eden

INTRODUCTION

My approach to food, entertaining, and life

is part of my DNA. My husband and I come from large, tight-knit families. We grew up in unique and powerful food cultures where flavors, family gatherings, and enjoying life were all interconnected. Where we come from, meals are a collective experience. Good food served with style to people you care about strengthens the wonderful bonds that join us all.

I wanted to make things that are easy for you, though. So, you'll find a gold mine of my own special occasion menus at the end of this book. Use that as an entertaining planner. Swap your favorites in as you see fit. As with the recipes themselves, look to make the menus your own. Enjoy the cooking, enjoy the flavors, and enjoy the people you share them with. That's the whole point.

I want this book to empower *anyone* to be a welcoming and creative cook and host—to share meals and create memories. The way I prepare food and entertain can best be described as relaxed elegance. Make every gathering a celebration. Find beauty wherever you can. The way we cook, eat, and entertain is an invitation to press pause, share, laugh, and come together. It's memories in the making. It's love.

Once upon a time, all that magic happened in my grandma's kitchen, at my dad's Shabbat table, or at my in-laws' apartment on Riverside Drive. Now it's my family's turn. My husband Abe and I love hosting any occasion, from summer cocktail parties to Shabbat dinners to Thanksgiving feasts. We're both the oldest siblings in our families, so it was only natural that we'd assume the clan-wide hosting duties when they became too much for our parents.

I can't begin to tell you how much we love it. There's nothing better than bringing our family and friends together to share dishes from around the world with a good measure of style and flair. You know you're doing it right when people don't want to get up from the table.

As you go through the book, keep in mind that the recipes aren't set in stone. I'm an interior designer and I've staged a lot of real estate, so putting my own stamp on things is definitely my jam. Honestly? I dress to suit my mood, and I have the same approach to cooking. I trust my gut, and I'm not afraid to try out new flavor combinations or different ingredients even when I'm cooking something I've made a million times before. Be fearless with anything you cook, but especially with whatever you make out of this book.

These recipes are forgiving and adaptable. They can be scaled up to suit whatever size crowd you're feeding. More than that, though, think of them as canvases for creativity and personalization. You're cooking in your own kitchen, so you might as well make the food all your own. I've been careful to pick recipes that aren't unreasonably complicated. Most of these dishes are "weeknight doable," although I want to help those of you who do not cook during Shabbat, too.

I've made things just as hassle-free for you by organizing the recipes and entertaining advice into common sense chapters, breakfast to dessert, but most of my dishes also bridge the gap from meal to meal. My famous and filling shakshuka (page 48) goes from brunch to dinner without batting an eye or losing a beat. Need a grab-and-go morning starter? How about the easy-peasy egg bites on page 40? You can just as conveniently add them to a cocktail-party tapas spread. And many of my desserts also work for a brunch as well as at the end of a meal. A good number of these recipes make super-satisfying snacks—and if you have a house full of kids, as I do, you know how important snacks can be.

The truth, though? We don't live by food alone. Okay, yes, we could. But how much more satisfying is food when it's served and enjoyed in a festive, lively, social atmosphere? I think everything tastes better when shared.

At the end of each chapter, you will find sections called "Make it Happen," which are my favorite ideas for taking every gathering to the next level and beyond. Let me guide you through every detail of managing occasions that showcase your own personal sense of style, while keeping the hosting part stress-free and fulfilling. I've included options for setting the perfect table, ways to rock an eye-catching bar setup, creative strategies to set exactly the mood you're after, and so much more.

Through this book, with me by your side, encouraging you with whispers in your ear, you will be the kind of host that gives parties that make memories.

KICHEN BASICS

Let's start with making sure you have the essential gear, supplies, and a thoughtfully stocked pantry like I have in my own kitchen. That way, all you will worry about is the cooking and socializing. Because special occasions should be just as enjoyable for the host as they are for the guests, am I right?

Most days I'm running from the moment I roll out of bed to whenever I finally call it a night. I don't need food prep to be another part of the grind. Quite the opposite. Making great meals should be as chill as possible. Ideally, it's even fun. To make this happen, I have collected super-useful kitchen tools and keep my pantry well stocked. So, let's make sure your kitchen is dressed for success.

Crucial Cookware

Kitchen gear is all the rage. I get that. It's so easy to be seduced by a slick cooking show and think, *"Wow, I got to get me one of those countertop pizza ovens."* No. No, you don't. Especially not in small, city apartments. My favorite tools are well-made and well-worn. Quality is going to cost you, but you're paying for ease of use and longevity.

Personally, I find prepping by hand a blessing. The time I spend making a meal is much-needed decompression. (Usually with some good tunes and wine to drown out my kids in the background!) Chopping vegetables with a knife or kneading dough by hand takes me back to that wonderful, fragrant, happy place that was my grandma's kitchen. Prep is also meditation under another name. It calms me down and helps me unwind from what are always jam-packed days. So, although I don't rely on a lot of fancy choppers and processors, I do need the best-in-class tools to get the job done as hassle-free as possible.

BLENDER

An indispensable appliance for pulverizing ingredients for condiments, purees, dips, and more. While a heavy-duty blender (such as a Vitamix) is great for its large-capacity jar, a standard blender works well, too. If your jar is plastic, whenever you work with chiles, rinse the jar out immediately so the oil doesn't stain the jar.

CAST-IRON SKILLET

You can't do better than a deep, cast-iron skillet when it comes to maintaining precise temperature control while cooking. I think everyone should own the traditional 12-inch (30.5cm) version for everyday use, but I also strongly recommend a larger 15-inch (38cm) version for big, family-style meals. As you use a cast-iron skillet, it absorbs the cooking fats to create a nonstick surface referred to as its "seasoning." You treat the skillet to keep the seasoning intact.

To clean cast iron, use a dry cloth to wipe out any cooking residue. Burnt-on bits? Nothing works like a spurtle (see what I did there?) to scrape the skillet clean. If that doesn't do the trick, add about a ¼ cup of warm water and a handful of kosher salt to the pan, and scrub with a stainless-steel scrubbing pad or kitchen sponge, letting the salt act like a scouring agent. Rinse, dry, and then heat on the stove over high heat to dry any residual water. You don't want to clean with soap, as that will remove the seasoning. If that happens, rub the inside of the skillet with vegetable oil and bake in a 350°F (180°C) oven for 1 hour to re-season the pan.

ENAMELED CAST-IRON COOKWARE

An enameled cast-iron Dutch oven is pricey but it's likely to last decades. My Le Creuset 6-quart version is one of my most treasured possessions. I also use their casserole dishes, which are perfect eye candy for any dinner or party.

KNIVES

This is probably the most important kitchen purchase you'll make. Buy high-quality and they will last a lifetime. High-carbon, stainless steel blades are easy to sharpen and care for, but always hand wash and dry knives right after use and never put them in the dishwasher.

The basic knives you'll use for most tasks are a 10-inch (25cm) chef's knife with a carbon stainless steel blade and a shorter 6- to 8-inch (15 to 20cm) version. They feel well-balanced in your hand. Your set should also include a 4-inch (10cm) paring knife, a 10-inch (25cm) serrated knife and, ideally, a thin 12-inch (30.5cm) slicing knife.

MIXING BOWLS

Such a simple thing, but so incredibly useful. You can never have too many. Stainless steel bowls won't break and are impervious to extreme temperatures.

MORTAR AND PESTLE

I don't own a food processor. I like the Old Skool version—the mortar and pestle. No shade against the processor. If you like yours, more power to you. But I appreciate the feeling of the heft of the pestle in my hand. You can use it to crush nuts for baking, and grind spices for spice blends. It crushes the ingredients instead of pulverizing them, giving them a better texture. To clean, mash up some raw rice or sugar in the mortar to pick up residue, and then wipe it out with a clean, dry cloth. Follow up with a moist cloth, if you wish, but be sure to dry it afterward.

SPURTLE

This is my all-in-one champion, a combination of a flat spatula, mixing paddle, and kitchen spoon. Spurtles come in lots of different sizes and materials (I can't live without my cherrywood version from Mad Hungry.).

MUFFIN PAN

You can use your muffin pan for much more than just muffins, such as Grandma's Crustless Quiche Tartlets (page 47) and Egg Bites (page 40). I am talking about the typical 12-cup pan. You might even want two of them. Be sure to have liners handy, too.

STAND MIXER

Yes, it's an investment, but once you have one you will be happy you took the plunge. They are especially good for kneading bread dough, leaving your hands free to do other things in the kitchen. (But I love the zen of kneading by hand, too . . . don't get me wrong!)

THE EXTRAS

Small kitchen essentials can elevate style while serving a purpose. Start with the humble BUTTER DISH. Basic designs include ceramic French butter cloches and crocks meant to hold spreadable butter. (I made mine with my daughter at a pottery class, and it's the one I still use in our kitchen.) SALT CELLARS keep an everyday staple close at hand, literally, and you can pick up the salt with your fingers for sprinkling. Ceramic or glass OLIVE OIL CRUETS offer the perfect combination of color, form, and function. All these items transition seamlessly between kitchen counter and dining room table.

The Perfectly Packed Pantry

It doesn't matter if you have a walk-in pantry (lucky you!) or just operate out of a few dedicated cupboards—staying well stocked up on the staples you use most often makes for hassle-free, successful cooking and entertaining.

IN THE PANTRY

SPICES

My favorite recipes are family treasures from the Middle East and Cuba, therefore the spices in my kitchen represent these cuisines and others. Some of these may be new to you, but I hope you get to know and love them as I do. I keep my spices organized in jars in a kitchen drawer, the rows separated by inserts, and labeled so that they are easier to read.

- Aleppo Pepper
- Cayenne Pepper
- Garlic Salt
- Ground Cardamon
- Ground Coriander
- Ground Cinnamon
- Ground Cumin
- Ground Turmeric
- Sweet Paprika
- Sumac

SPICE BLENDS

These are the secret ingredients that take cooking to another level, mixing a few spices so they become a sum greater than their parts. Some of them can be made at home instead of purchasing at the store.

Adobo: A staple in Latin cooking, this dry seasoning (there is liquid adobo, too) has a salt base with garlic, onion, paprika, and more.

Baharat: Yemenite cooks reach for this wonderful spice blend of "warm" spices often, and so do I. (Recipe on page 98.)

Everything Bagel Seasoning: This is the topping on New York's world famous everything bagel, with sesame seeds, poppy seeds, and dried bits of garlic and onion. It makes a wonderful topping for all kinds of breads, not just bagels.

Harissa: A brick-red, very spicy North African paste blend that is sold in jars and very convenient tubes.

Hawaij: Another traditional Yemenite spice blend, it's earthy with a distinctive yellow color from turmeric. (Recipe on page 98.)

Za'atar: Fragrant with an oregano-like aroma, this is *the* spice blend in the Middle East and fast becoming a top choice in American kitchens, as well. (Recipe on page 98.)

BOUILLON PASTE

A quality bouillon can make all the difference in soups or stews. I use Better than Bouillon, which is a paste. It adds a deep rich flavor that other forms just don't.

SOUP CROUTONS (MANDELS)

Crunchy and irresistible, these mini croutons go in soups.

OILS

Welcome to the golden age of culinary oils. Green, cold-pressed extra virgin olive oil remains my go-to for recipes, sauces, dressings, and dipping. I'm a big fan of the Graza brand, which sells two versions in handy squeeze bottles—one for cooking, and one for drizzling onto pastas, proteins, or into dressings and sauces.

Olive oil, though, is just the start. Avocado oil has a lighter, more delicate flavor.

BASMATI RICE
My family loves rice, especially this aromatic long-grain variety that is a favorite in the Middle East and India.

ROSEWATER
A very flowery liquid used to flavor desserts and my homemade grenadine.

SALTS
I use Maldon flaky sea salt, which is unadulterated and has a very clean taste, for most of my cooking. I usually stick to the plain Maldon salt, but there are also flavored versions like garlic, chili, and smoked, which are great for seasoning a dish right before serving. I also use Celtic as a general, all-around option. However, kosher salt is the little black cocktail dress of cooking salts, preferably Diamond Crystal brand in the familiar red box. I always taste at intervals as I cook to gradually build to the final seasoning.

IN THE FRIDGE
I am a condiments person, and my fridge is full of surprises. I like making my own versions of some condiments because then I'm in control of the food that my family puts in their bodies. On any given day, here's what you'll find in my refrigerator, just waiting to be turned into great meals for friends and family.

CHEESE
Tangy sheep's milk feta has a crumbly texture that is unique in the cheese world. While supermarket feta is good, if you come across wet-packed bulk feta in brine at a delicatessen or cheese store, you'll be able to tell the difference. (I even use splashes of the brine as an ingredient.) Semi-hard cheeses like Cheddar and Gruyère should be kept on hand for shredding to be used in recipes and for snacking. Grating cheese, such as good old Parmesan, is another must-have.

KETCHUP
Make your own (see page 92) and you'll never buy the bottled version again.

MAYONNAISE
Another condiment that's easy to make at home. (Recipe on page 93.)

OLIVES
I keep a stock of versatile, satisfying olives for cooking and snacking. My stash includes (pitted and whole) kalamata, plump Castelvetrano, and a Greek olive mix.

SCHUG
Also called zhug (or variations thereof), this thick pesto-like spread comes in green (cilantro-based) and red (chilies and garlic). It's supposed to be pretty hot, so don't let its mellow look fool you. (See my recipes on page 104.)

TAHINI/TAHINA
You can find tahini, the thick sesame paste, at supermarkets, but superior brands are often sold at Middle Eastern delicatessens. With a few additions, it becomes the silky, flavor-rich sauce known as tahina (see page 101).

ERIN'S NEW YORK CITY

PARTY PARADISE

I'm a New York City hometown girl and I love to take advantage of the unique treasures the city has to offer. So, I thought I'd show you around my favorite places for one-of-kind food, drinks, and entertaining supplies. Most of these hot spots have websites, so even if you don't live in the Big Apple you can still take a bite out of it.

DELICATESSENS

There's a great deli on just about every corner of my city, but a couple of superstars hold a special place in my heart and cooking.

ZABAR'S

This beloved NYC institution is the world's best deli, but it's so much more than that. Zabar's is part mouthwatering grocery store, part catering resource, and part epic traditional delicatessen. They have anything you might need for your party's food, and everything is enticingly delicious. Zabar's sells both prepared and raw ingredients—all of the highest quality. The store is most famous for authentic ethnic specialties like babka, smoked fish of all kinds, and braided challah. But they also have one of the most incredible artisanal cheese selections you'll ever find. My absolute fave product at Zabar's is their smoked salmon, because of how incredibly thin they slice it.

EATALY

The name says it all—a mashup of "eat" and "Italy." The aisles of Eataly contain one-of-a-kind gems, like unique and exceptional twenty-five-year-old balsamic vinegars, rare black truffles, and spectacular cured meats, including to-die-for prosciutto. Order any of those directly online, but if you shop at Eataly in person, you can get their incredible bread and pasta.

MURRAY'S STURGEON

Another Upper West Side kosher deli that's been around for generations, Murray's is a shoe-box-sized version of Zabar's, and it has its die-hard fans, too. Smoked fish of all kinds is the reason to come here.

BARNEY GREENGRASS

We New Yorkers love our breakfasts and brunches. For many of us, there is no better way to enjoy these meals than at Barney's, a restaurant that also sells its goods by the pound. A bagel topped with their lox, a hot coffee, a table of friends and family—that is a Manhattanite food-lover's heaven.

GROCERIES & PROVISIONS

WHOLE FOODS

It might not be a New York City native, but Whole Foods embodies the high-bar standards the city demands. The Bowery branch even has two levels, and the Columbus Circle location is huge, too! The attraction for me is all about freshness and selection. The store focuses on organic options and takes care to stock the best produce you can find outside of a New York City farmer's market.

KALUSTYAN'S SPICES

Tucked away in the Murray Hill neighborhood, this is a spice emporium that runs the gamut from the everyday to the exotic, all of the very best quality. They have their own baharat and hawaij, or you can get the ingredients to make your versions. Whenever you're looking for an unusual ingredient, check here first.

FAIRWAY

There are people who would argue that the best reason to move to the Upper West Side is the proximity to two of this market's locations, one far north and the other at the south end. Originally a produce store, now it carries a little of everything, and is especially known for its cheese and coffee selection.

PRODUCE

For the most tightly packed urban area in the country, New York City is blessed with more than its share of stellar farmer's markets. Most are open one day a week and offer not only fresh-from-the-farm produce, but exceptional meat, fish, poultry, and even specialty farm products like different flavors of raw honey. Two of the best are the Union Square Market downtown and the year-round 79th Street Greenmarket that expands in-season to a stretch of Columbus Avenue from 77th to 81st Streets. The produce is out of this world, and you can find specialized growers tucked away in smaller booths, offering interesting and unusual products like fresh-grown wasabi and garlic scapes.

CHELSEA MARKET

Located in a former biscuit factory on the edge of the chic neighborhood of Chelsea, this ultra-cool location is packed with small, fun shops where you can get everything from boutique chocolates to a bespoke taco. I usually go straight to the Manhattan Fruit Market. They offer an incredible selection of just-picked-fresh produce. I like it because no matter what fruit or veggie you're dreaming of, you're likely to find it here—from chocolate basil to purple carrots to eye-catching dragon fruit. And they also carry a gorgeous selection of freshly squeezed fruit juice—perfect for when you have to mix up big batches of Mezcalitas (see page 189).

MEATS & POULTRY

HUDSON & CHARLES

First and foremost, they're a butcher. This is my favorite place to buy high-quality meats and poultry. That said, Hudson & Charles is more than just a butcher shop. They stock an amazing variety of specialty items. They also support home-grown vendors, and offer local beers, ciders, cheeses, and other "New York–first" products. Add to that a variety of novel prepared goods and is it any wonder this store is high on my list of city gems?

PRIME CUT

This is my absolute first choice for kosher proteins. The market offers a wide variety of meats, poultry, and cuts, and they make the best spinach-chicken burgers on earth. They even sell packaged hot dogs (chicken franks and beef dogs) and deli items. All are super high quality and incredibly delicious. They are well worth the trip out to the Gravesend neighborhood of Brooklyn, or you can order them online directly.

BREADS & BAKED GOODS

MICHAELI BAKERY

This Upper East Side treasure creates the most incredible traditional Israeli baked goods you can imagine. Legendary babka, melt-on-the-tongue rugalach, perfect challah, and more.

BREADS BAKERY

For a downtown location (they also have stores all over town) that sells Israeli-style baked goods, check out the Union Square location of Breads. It's the perfect place to break a New Year's resolution to cut back on carbs.

ORWASHERS

If you're a fan of Eastern European rye breads, look no further than their original location in Yorkville, where many immigrants settled. Their pumpernickel is the real deal. They have five locations and mail order, too.

CAPUTO'S BAKE SHOP

Brooklyn is packed with little Italian bakeries. It seems like there's one on every corner—for good reason, because there *is* one on every corner. Well, almost. But the best of them stay around forever. Caputo's has been doing business since the Dodgers were a Brooklyn team, and the bakery is just a short F train ride from Manhattan into that borough's Carroll Gardens neighborhood. They bake their bread daily, and you'll find all the classics here rainbow cookies, prosciutto bread (just like it sounds!), biscotti, Italian horns, cannoli, and sfogliatelle. They don't have a website so it's the perfect excuse to come to New York City for a visit!

DESSERTS

MAGNOLIA

You probably know them as the cupcake place from *Sex and the City*, and they certainly bake up life-changing cupcakes. They don't stop, there, though. Magnolia makes transcendent mini cheesecakes, killer brownies and blondies, and exceptional pudding. More often than not, I stop by to pick up one of their classically flavored and perfectly yummy full-size cakes for a birthday or other special occasion (like, say, Shabbat).

WINE & LIQUOR

ASTOR WINE & SPIRITS

There are few liquor stores that can rival Astor's selection of wine and booze—in or out of New York City. The store occupies a cavernous Lower East Side location. If you're a fan of wines and other spirits from around the world, you can get lost in the aisles for days. They also carry Mezcalum!

COCKTAIL KINGDOM

Turn to these guys for a stunning selection of cocktail-mixing hardware, such as shakers and strainers in finishes like copper, brass, and gunmetal black. They also offer chic bar knives and a wide variety of different cocktail glasses, including tumblers, mezcal glasses, and really cool rocks glasses. They even stock funky tiki glassware and zombie glasses.

TABLETOP

Honestly? I have two tried-and-true resources for unique and eye-catching tabletop décor: Amazon and Etsy. I know they're not native New Yorkers, but they offer huge searchable collections of things you might not find anywhere else. Shop them for unique votive candleholders, one-of-a-kind small serving bowls and dishes, and handmade napkin rings. These are great resources for inexpensive accessories that can add bling to your next hosted event.

FLOWERS

FLOWER DISTRICT

This not-so-hidden treasure is a favorite of bloom-loving New Yorkers, on 28th Street, between 6th and 7th Avenues. You can find just about any flower in pretty much any quantity you could ever want or need. It's the perfect resource if you're planning a big get-together and, for instance, want to create a stunning tabletop packed with pink peonies (say that three times fast!).

PLANTSHED

I could happily lose myself for a day in this florist and coffee shop offering an amazing variety of flowers and incredible coffee (doesn't hurt that they're right in my Upper West Side neighborhood!). Whether you're after sensational ready-made centerpiece arrangements, unique and delicate orchids, or spectacular candles, this is the place! The perfumed air alone makes it worth visiting. One of the things I love the most is that they match candles to floral bouquets.

1

BREAKFAST *and* BRUNCH

Breakfast HOLDS A SPECIAL PLACE IN *my heart.*

On Sunday mornings, Dad (aka Abba) would take me to the Triangle Diner on First (Street) and First (Avenue) at the edge of Manhattan's Lower East Side. I'd order Malawach (page 52) with powdered sugar and Dad would have a Turkish coffee with Jachnun (page 55) or Shakshuka (page 48). Sitting across from Abba was so much more than just a meal, it was a firstborn, father-daughter moment and a keepsake mental snapshot. That's the best any breakfast can be.

I recreate that vibe with my own kids during weekend breakfasts in the Hamptons. I love starting my mornings with my oldest, ten-year-old Levi. Breakfast is the ideal meal for him to work on his cooking game. It's fun experimenting together by putting our own spin on my grandma's tried-and-true Quiche (page 47) or Abba's fave Jachnun. It's also a group thing. His brother and sister help out by kneading the dough, setting the table, and adding a happy background soundtrack of chatter and laughter.

Those weekend breakfasts are a big part of how I recharge when I need it the most. I come back to the city ready to tackle whatever the week might hold in store for me.

Lovely as that all is, I don't think I have to tell you that long, leisurely restorative breakfasts are just not possible every day. Chances are, you're like me. Your days start in a sprint. You have to get ready for work or shoot out to the gym for a quick sweat sesh. In my case, I have FOUR little humans to corral. Find that missing homework and make sure the jacket someone's wearing (or not wearing) matches the weather forecast.

It's a lot. Life is hectic and it's easy to lose sight of the first and most important purpose of breakfast: to supply nutritious and filling fuel for the day. A bowl of sugar bombs floating in two percent milk ain't going to cut it, not to mention my health nut mom would be horrified. Much as I love the slow pace and flavor-packed nature of my shakshuka, I lean heavy on my portable egg bites and the hidden nutrition and fiber in the Banana Spinach Muffins (page 39). These grab-and-go packages deliver a satisfying, healthy breakfast.

Brunch is breakfast's slower, richer sibling—a meal that is not in a hurry. Brunch is a party—an early party, but a celebration, nonetheless. Quenching thirst is as important as filling bellies, and it's going to require something more than just great coffee (although the coffee you serve should be fantastic). For me, that means something a little boozy! Lighter spirits and wines are the order of the day, along with the occasional filling Bloody Mary (I love to have one to hold me over for the meal), and any brunch table worth its salt should include fresh juices for drinking and mixing.

Ultimately, though, whether it's breakfast or brunch, the occasion always starts with feeding yourself and your clan great, wholesome food.

GREEK YOGURT
with Roasted Stone Fruit and Almonds

I feel incredibly grateful that Abe proposed to me on the drop-dead gorgeous Greek island of Santorini. Everything about that getaway was magnificent and memorable. Along with about a million memories (and photos), I brought back an incredibly simple new breakfast habit. Every morning, on a patio overlooking the Aegean Sea, I would start the day with thick Greek yogurt with different fruits and nuts in it, topped off with fresh honey. So delicious. It's also incredibly healthy for the stomach. (Ladies, at the risk of offering TMI, we'll say it's remarkably beneficial for gut health. You're welcome.) You can substitute all kinds of seasonal fruit and your favorite nuts but take my word for it: roasting fruit elevates breakfast to a whole new level and just looks stunning.

PREP: **10 minutes**   COOK: **25 to 30 minutes**

1 pound (454g) *fresh apricots*, *peaches*, *plums,* or other stone fruit, halved and pitted, or halved and stemmed figs

1 tablespoon *organic raw honey*, plus more for serving

Ground cinnamon and/or ground cardamom, for sprinkling (optional)

1× 48-ounce (1.3kg) container *plain Greek yogurt*

½ cup coarsely chopped *roasted, salted almonds* (any nut will do, I sometimes love mixed nuts, chopped)

1. Preheat the oven to 350°F (180°C). Arrange the apricots cut-side up in a single layer in a baking dish and drizzle with honey. Lightly sprinkle with the cinnamon, if using.

2. Bake until the apricots caramelize and brown around the edges and are tender when pierced with the tip of a sharp knife, 25 to 30 minutes. Transfer to a wire rack to cool completely. The apricots can be stored in a tightly sealed container in the refrigerator for up to one week.

3. For each serving, spoon about ¾ cup of the yogurt into a cereal or soup bowl. Top with 2 or 3 apricot halves and a scattering of chopped nuts. Drizzle with honey and serve.

Healthy
PANCAKE STICKS

As a mom to hungry kids, there's never a downside to making food fun. And few things I make are more fun than this breakfast treat. My kids used to drown a stack of regular pancakes in syrup, leaving a sticky mess everywhere in the kitchen . . . and beyond. I am a neat freak so that didn't work well for me. I found the answer by making the pancakes into handheld dip-and-eat sticks. I keep them high fiber by using whole wheat flour. If you want to dial back the sugar, make the chocolate chips optional. No matter how you make yours, though, this recipe is incredibly easy and quick, no pancake mix needed. Another plus for any busy mom!

PREP: **15 minutes**   COOK: **15 minutes**

1⅔ cups *whole wheat flour* or unbleached all-purpose flour, plus more as needed

¼ cup *granulated sugar*

1½ teaspoons *baking powder*

1 teaspoon *kosher salt*

1 cup *whole milk*

4 tablespoons *unsalted butter*, melted and cooled

2 large *eggs*

1 teaspoon *pure vanilla extract*

½ cup *mini chocolate chips* (optional)

Vegetable oil, for the skillet

Butter and *pure maple syrup*, for serving (optional)

1. Preheat the oven to 200°F (95°C). In a large mixing bowl, whisk the flour, sugar, baking powder, and salt. In a small mixing bowl, whisk the milk, butter, eggs, and vanilla. Pour into the flour mixture and stir until just combined; a few lumps are fine. The batter should be a little thicker than regular pancake batter to ensure the sticks aren't floppy; add flour 1 tablespoon at a time if necessary to thicken. Stir in the mini chocolate chips, if desired.

2. Stand an opened 1-gallon (3.8 liters) resealable plastic bag inside of a tall jar or drinking glass, with the open end cuffed over the edge of the glass to stabilize it. Scrape the batter into the open bag and seal it, pushing out as much air as possible. Refrigerate at least 15 minutes.

3. Heat a large nonstick skillet over medium heat. Drizzle it with vegetable oil and use a paper towel to spread the oil evenly across the pan.

4. Snip a bottom corner off the bag about ¼ inch (6mm) in from the corner (Levi's brilliant idea!). Pipe the batter through the hole onto the skillet, piping out sticks about ¾ inch (18mm) wide and 3 to 4 inches (7 to 10cm) long. Pipe as many sticks as you can fit on the surface without them touching. Don't crowd the sticks, as they will expand slightly. Cook until bubbles form and pop on the surface of the sticks and the bottoms are golden brown, about 2 minutes. Flip and cook until browned on the other side, about 1 minute. Transfer to a platter if serving immediately or keep warm in the oven on a baking sheet while cooking the remaining pancake sticks.

5. Serve with butter and ramekins of maple syrup for dipping. The cooled pancakes can be refrigerated in an airtight container for up to 4 days. Or freeze the pancakes on a baking sheet until firm, transfer to a resealable plastic bag, and freeze for up to 1 month. Thaw the frozen pancakes at room temperature for 30 minutes to 1 hour. To reheat, bake in a preheated 350°F (180°C) oven or on a tray in a toaster oven for about 5 minutes.

TORREJAS

This version of French toast made its way from Spain—where it's a traditional and beloved breakfast for Lent—to Mexico, Latin America, and Cuba (where Abe's relatives first made it part of their morning ritual). It's simple, filling, and quick to make. I typically use leftover challah instead of the classic doughy Cuban sobao bread or the Mexican bolillo. You can use French bread in a pinch. Stay away from plain white bread, which won't be as flavorful and also is just not good for ya! The most important part, though, is that the bread is slightly stale, so it becomes a sponge for the wet ingredients and flavors. Speaking of flavors, you can opt for the classic olive oil rather than vegetable oil (I find the flavor has a subtly bitter edge that is interesting, but my kids don't love it as much). I strongly recommend you experiment, and maybe go a little wild, with the toppings. We serve it with maple syrup, but in Spain, they're just as likely to use warmed molasses, honey, or even just a dusting of cinnamon sugar.

PREP: **15 minutes**   _COOK:_ **15 minutes**

1-pound (454g) loaf **challah bread**, preferably stale

1½ cups **whole milk**, warmed

¼ cup (50g) **granulated sugar**

1 teaspoon **ground cinnamon**

¼ teaspoon **ground nutmeg**

Pinch of **ground star anise** or cloves (optional)

3 large **eggs**

2 tablespoons **vegetable** or **olive oil**, for frying, plus more as needed

2 tablespoons **salted** or **unsalted butter**, plus more as needed

TOPPINGS
Warmed **maple syrup**, **honey**, or **agave**

Whipped cream

Cinnamon sugar

1. Preheat the oven to 200°F (95°C). Cut the bread into 1-inch (2.5cm) slices. In a large shallow bowl, whisk the milk, sugar, cinnamon, nutmeg, and star anise (if using) to dissolve the sugar. In a second shallow bowl, beat the eggs until uniform.

2. Line a baking sheet or platter with paper towels and place it next to the stovetop. In a large nonstick frying pan over medium-high heat, heat the oil with the butter until sizzling. Working with one slice of bread at a time, dip both sides in the milk mixture (whisk it quickly first to reincorporate the spices for stronger flavor), then dip both sides in the egg. Let the excess run off quickly and place the slice in the hot pan. Repeat with as many slices as will fit in the pan at one time without crowding. Fry until golden brown and crispy on the bottom, about 2 minutes. Flip and cook until golden brown and crispy on the other side, about 2 minutes more. Transfer to the baking sheet or platter and keep warm in the oven until all the torrejas are cooked. Add more butter and oil as needed.

3. Serve warm with a generous amount of warm maple syrup or agave, whipped cream, or your favorite topping.

BANANA SPINACH MUFFINS

This is a hidden nutrition recipe. I pack so much spinach into these and my kids have no idea, thanks to the deep, rich sweetness of the bananas. But I personally love them, too, and they're great for babies because of how soft they are. The recipe is reliable just as it is, but I know that some people aren't wild about whole wheat flour. (I use it to give my kids a big blast of fiber in their diet. Another thing they're in the dark about!) If you're not a fan, replace one cup of the whole wheat flour with one cup of all-purpose. They'll taste more like regular muffins but still be mega healthy. While bananas and walnuts go together (my personal preference), I sometimes leave them out because the muffins often go to school with my kids and you never want to risk triggering another kid's nut allergy. Use the plant-based options to make these dairy free.

PREP: **15 minutes**   *COOK:* **20 to 25 minutes**
TOTAL: **35 to 40 minutes**

2 cups **whole wheat flour**
1 teaspoon **baking powder**
1 teaspoon **baking soda**
1 teaspoon **ground cinnamon**
1 teaspoon **kosher salt**
5 ounces (140g) **baby spinach** (about 4 packed cups)
¾ cup **maple syrup** or 1 cup granulated sugar
1 cup **whole milk** or almond milk
½ cup **unsalted butter**, melted and cooled, or coconut oil
1 cup ripe mashed **bananas** (about 3 large bananas)
3 large **eggs**
1 cup coarsely chopped **walnuts** (optional)
1 cup **mini chocolate chips** (optional)

Special Equipment: Two standard 12-cup muffin tins and paper or silicone muffin liners

1. Preheat the oven to 350°F (180°C). Line the cups of two 12-cup muffin pans with liners.

2. In a medium mixing bowl, whisk together the flour, baking powder, baking soda, cinnamon, and salt. If using sugar (not maple syrup), add it to the bowl with the dry ingredients.

3. In this order, to a blender jar, add the spinach, maple syrup (if using), milk, butter or coconut oil, bananas, and eggs. Blend until smooth. Add to the bowl with the flour mixture and stir until just combined. There will be a few lumps! Gently stir in the walnuts and chocolate chips (if using).

4. Divide the batter among the muffin cups. (I use an ice cream scoop.) Bake until a toothpick inserted in the center of a muffin comes out with a few crumbs, 20 to 25 minutes.

5. Let cool in the pan for 10 minutes, then transfer the muffins to a wire rack to cool completely. The cooled muffins can be refrigerated in an airtight container for up to 3 days, or frozen for up to 1 month.

GO, TEAM!

This is a great recipe for getting kids involved. I let mine mash up the bananas. They love the squishy texture, and it keeps them busy forever! They also think it is fun using an ice cream scoop to fill the cups with batter. If you want only some muffins with walnuts (or chocolate chips), add half the amount of nuts to the batter after you've filled half the muffin cups. Put a walnut half (or a few chips) on top of each of the cups that have them to identify after baking.

EGG BITES

These protein-packed wonders are proof positive that dynamite comes in small packages. I regularly make these for a quick breakfast and grab-and-go snacks. One of the best things about the recipe is that you can substitute for just about any ingredient except the eggs. Use whatever cheese floats your boat, or throw in onions, garlic, or veggies left over from another recipe. And it's a blank canvas for your favorite herbs and seasonings. Of course, these are also perfect finger food for a brunch spread, or dust them with smoked paprika and chives for an easy platter filler when you're doing a night of tapas!

PREP: **20 minutes**   COOK: **25 to 30 minutes**

Nonstick cooking spray

1 pound (454g) **lean ground beef** (about 90% lean, such as sirloin)

¾ teaspoon **kosher salt**, divided

2 **broccoli crowns** (about 1 pound [454g])

12 large **eggs**

1 teaspoon **adobo seasoning**

1 teaspoon **garlic powder**

½ teaspoon freshly ground **black pepper**

1 cup crumbled **feta** or 2 cups shredded sharp Cheddar

Special Equipment: Two standard 12-cup muffin tins

1. Preheat the oven to 375°F (190°C). Generously grease the cups of two nonstick 12-cup muffin pans with cooking spray.

2. Bring a large pot of salted water to a boil over high heat.

3. Meanwhile, to a large skillet over medium heat, add the beef and ¼ teaspoon salt. Break up the meat with the side of a wooden spoon, and cook until browned, about 4 minutes. Using a slotted spoon, transfer the beef to a medium mixing bowl.

4. Add the broccoli to the pot of boiling water and cook until it turns bright green and just begins to soften, about 2 minutes. Place a large mixing bowl with ice and cold water next to the stovetop. Using tongs, transfer the broccoli to the ice bath with tongs and let cool. Drain the broccoli well. Cut the florets off the stalk of each crown and coarsely chop the florets. Add the chopped broccoli to the beef and mix.

5. In another large mixing bowl, whisk the eggs, adobo, garlic powder, ½ teaspoon salt, and the pepper until uniform. Stir in the cheese with the beef and broccoli mixture. Divide the mixture evenly among the cups of the muffin pans (I use an ice-cream scoop).

6. Bake until the bites are firm, 25 to 30 minutes. If you want them more brown and crisped on top, broil them in the pans about 6 inches (15cm) from the heat, about 1 minute. (Watch them carefully because they can easily burn.)

7. Transfer the pan to a wire rack and let cool for 5 minutes. Remove the bites from the muffin pan and serve warm or cool completely. The egg bites can be refrigerated in an airtight container for up to 2 days. Or freeze them in a resealable plastic bag for up to 1 month. Reheat in a microwave oven for 30 seconds to 1 minute, depending on whether they are refrigerated or frozen.

SABICH

Even though it has eggplant instead of fried garbanzo bean balls, I like to call this a breakfast version of falafel pita. (Of course it makes a fine lunch, too.) The idea is to have all of the various components in the fridge to throw it together on the go.

PREP: **10 minutes**   COOK: **5 minutes, to warm the pita**

4 *pita bread*s
Hummus (see page 99)
Fried Eggplant (see page 95)
4 *Shabbat Eggs* (see page 44), or hard-boiled eggs, peeled and sliced lengthwise
Tahina (see page 101)
Israeli Salad (see page 75)
Schug (see page 104) (optional)

1. Preheat the oven or a toaster oven to 225°F (110°C). Heat the pita in the oven to warm them, about 5 minutes.

2. Cut the top from each pita to create a pocket. For each sabich, smear a few tablespoons of hummus into a pita. Add several fried eggplant and egg slices. Drizzle with a little tahina, then add a generous spoonful of Israeli salad. Drizzle with some more tahina and schug, if desired, and serve.

MAKES
12
eggs

SHABBAT EGGS
(Haminados)

I often make Shabbat eggs as part of another recipe, but then there's my Aunt Susan's stand-alone slow-cooker method, which she swears by and only needs a crock pot (or any pot) of water... and time. She prefers cooking them for two (!) nights to give them an even deeper color and flavor.

PREP: **5 minutes**   *COOK:* **36 to 48 hours**

12 large *eggs*
Kosher salt (optional)

Special Equipment: Slow cooker

1. Place the eggs in a single layer in a slow cooker. Add water to cover. Season generously with salt, if desired.

2. Cook on low for about 36 hours (over the course of two nights).

3. Drain the eggs and let them cool completely. (The eggs can be refrigerated in an airtight container for up to 1 week.)

SHARING My *Shabbat* Eggs

Shabbat eggs are a delicacy unlike any hardboiled egg you've ever tasted. That's because they're slow cooked for a long, long time instead of boiling for a few minutes, completely changing the flavor and its complexity. These are part of my family's Shabbat ritual and common to many Jewish families. Shabbat involves the period from sundown on Friday to sundown on Saturday, during which time religious laws restrict the use of machinery like stoves or kitchen appliances (and cars). Though we are not religious, Jewish families traditionally leave the oven on low overnight, to slow cook the next day's meal. A byproduct of this necessary cooking style is absolutely delicious food. I nestle the eggs in with my Shabbat chicken and leave it to cook for eight hours. There's not a lot more to it. The eggs just keep cooking little by little, right alongside the bird. We'll eat them the next day or even during the week. Don't get hung up on the name or the tradition; the idea works anytime you're cooking something low and slow, like the concept of smoking brisket or the Thanksgiving turkey. The eggs come out deep brown and my kids absolutely love them. They have a subtle nuttiness and can pick up some of the flavors from whatever they cook with. Short on time, or don't have plans to cook anything that long? You can still make Shabbat eggs without having to put them in the oven. Gently nestle them in a pot of water and cook them over a slow, low boil for 8 to 12 hours. Sometimes, I'll add onion skins and garlic cloves to the water to lend more flavor. Or do as my Aunt Susan does—cook them in a slow cooker on low for 36 to 48 hours. The longer the better!

Grandma's
CRUSTLESS QUICHE

My grandma had a talent for transforming simple dishes into special memories. This quiche is one of her gems—deeply satisfying, super nutritious, and so easy to make. She always made hers without the crust and, for the most part, so do I. It's a great way to enjoy all the flavor while sparing yourself the carbs. Crust or no, the best thing about quiche—especially my grandma's—is its versatility. There are so many ways you can adapt this for your own table and preferences. And my grandma's motto was, the cheesier the better. If you don't have my specific references for cheese, any cheese will do. And mix the cheeses up! Make this for brunch and you will find guests coming back to the table to nibble on it all day long. For that reason, it also makes a great weekend breakfast for families!

PREP: **20 to 25 minutes**   COOK: **45 to 55 minutes**

1× 16-ounce (454g) bag of *frozen chopped spinach*, thawed and squeezed to remove excess moisture

2 cups shredded *low-moisture mozzarella*, divided

1½ cups freshly grated *Parmesan*, divided

8 ounces (227g) *sheep's milk feta*, crumbled, plus 1 to 2 tablespoons of its brine (see Note)

8 large *eggs*, lightly beaten

¼ teaspoon *dried oregano*

¼ teaspoon *garlic powder*

¼ teaspoon *cayenne*

½ teaspoon *smoked paprika*

½ teaspoon *kosher salt*

¼ teaspoon freshly ground *black pepper*

1. Preheat the oven to 350°F (180°C). Lightly oil the bottom and sides of a 3-quart (3L) oblong casserole dish, about 9×13 inches (23×33cm).

2. In a large mixing bowl, mix the spinach, 1½ cups of the mozzarella, 1¼ cups of the Parmesan, feta, and its brine. Add the eggs, oregano, garlic powder, smoked paprika, salt, and pepper. Using a spoon (or your hands), mix well. Transfer to the casserole dish and smooth the top. Sprinkle the remaining mozzarella and Parmesan evenly across the top.

3. Bake until the top is golden brown and crispy, 45 to 55 minutes. Let cool slightly before serving.

VARIATIONS

CLASSIC QUICHE: Divide the filling between two 8-inch (20cm) frozen pie crusts and top with cheese as directed above. Place the quiches on a baking sheet and bake as directed. Don't want the pie tin clashing with your beautiful tablescape? Slip each baked quiche into an attractive ceramic pie plate.

QUICHE TARTLETS: Thaw 2× 14-ounce (397g) packages of frozen puff pastry (2 sheets). On a floured work surface, roll each sheet to roughly 9×12 inches (23×30cm). Cut each into 12 equal squares. Generously grease the cups in two 12-cup muffin tins. Fit 1 square into each cup. Divide the filling equally among the cups (I use an ice-cream scoop). Sprinkle each with mozzarella and parmesan as directed above. Bake until the tops are browned, 40 to 45 minutes. Let cool on a wire rack for about 5 minutes, then serve warm.

NOTE *Imported feta cheese is often sold packed in containers with brine. If you have a block of cheese without much brine, don't worry about it.*

SHAKSHUKA

Shakshuka. The impetus, and the heart, of this entire book! I have so many happy memories of this dish, both ones that I grew up with and ones I enjoyed on my own when hosting. There's a good reason why cultures from around the world—from rural Italians to Mexican vaqueros—make their own versions. It's a truly authentic dish that profoundly connects people. Everyone scooping out their own serving from the same communal dish becomes an intimate, shared moment that is the best part of the meal. While it is vegetarian, you could also add any type of sausage, ground beef, or even leftover roast chicken for a boost of texture and flavor. I like to add chopped kalamata olives and crumbled feta. The key is cooking the sauce for a long period of time as your patience will be rewarded with a healthy, delicious, and satisfying meal, especially when served with a crusty rustic loaf. I am a sourdough fanatic but when I'm trying to be "good" I'll have it with a variety of crackers.

PREP: **10 minutes** _COOK:_ **35 to 40 minutes**

1 **head garlic**, peeled, and thinly sliced (like in Goodfellas; about ⅓ cup total)

½ cup **extra virgin olive oil**, plus more as needed

3 to 4 medium **yellow onions**, finely chopped

1½ teaspoons **garlic powder** (or to taste)

1½ teaspoons **adobo seasoning**

½ teaspoon **cumin**

¼ teaspoon **cayenne powder** (optional)

Kosher salt and freshly ground **black pepper**

3 to 4 large ripe **tomatoes** roughly chopped or 1 cup additional marinara sauce

1½ cups **marinara sauce** (if I don't have my own stored, my go-to jarred faves are Rao's, Carbone, or Monte's Fine Foods)

8 to 10 large **eggs**

½ cup finely chopped **flat leaf parsley**

Feta, **olives**, or other topping of choice

Pita, sliced **sourdough bread**, sliced **baguette**, and/or **crackers** for serving

Special Equipment: 12- to 14-inch (30.5 to 35.5cm) heavy skillet, preferably cast iron (see Note)

1. Heat the oil and garlic together in a 12 to 14-inch (30.5cm to 35.5cm) cast-iron or heavy stainless-steel skillet over medium heat, stirring often, until golden, about 2 to 4 minutes. Watch it closely because the garlic can burn quickly. Add the onions and cook until golden and translucent, about 15 minutes.

2. Stir in the garlic powder, adobo seasoning, cumin, and cayenne (if using), and season with salt and pepper. Add the tomatoes (or marinara sauce) and continue to stir constantly. It will take roughly 10 minutes to cook down the tomatoes. Stir in the marinara sauce. Cook until thickened, roughly 5 minutes.

3. Using the back of a spoon, press 8 to 10 divots, equally spaced apart, into the sauce. One at a time, carefully crack the eggs into the sauce.

4. Sprinkle with half the parsley and/or feta, olives, if using. Cover and reduce the heat to medium-low. Simmer until the egg whites are set and the yolks reach your desired firmness (about 5 minutes for a soft yolk and 7 minutes for a firmer yolk). Keep in mind that the eggs will continue cooking a bit even after you remove them from the heat.

5. Scatter the remaining parsley for garnish and serve hot, right from the skillet, with your bread(s) of choice.

NOTE _While you can use a quality, heavy-bottom, stainless-steel skillet (I love my All-Clad!), I strongly recommend that you use cast iron. It heats uniformly, which is crucial to not burning the sauce during cooking. Just be sure that your cast-iron skillet is properly seasoned (see page 16) or the pan may give the food a metallic taste. I usually make this in a bigger batch (with 10 to 12 eggs) in my favorite skillet, which is about 15 inches (38cm) wide. Just increase the ingredients by about one quarter. It makes a terrific impression on guests when it comes to the table._

CHILAQUILES

I'm kind of obsessed with this dish. It's an easy and awesome thing to prepare, a south-of-the-border, chip-based alternative to my shakshuka. I serve it when I want to mix things up a little, especially for a summer brunch. It's also the absolute perfect partner for brunch-time Mezcalum cocktails, my favorite summer drink. Chilaquiles is an excellent option when friends or family drop by last minute for a late breakfast or brunch. It's quick to throw together and you can use whatever you have on hand—except for the tortilla chips. (True confession: I *always* have tortilla chips on hand.) The classic version doesn't include eggs, but I add them because I think they transform the dish from a hot dip into a true breakfast feast. They are easiest to eat from wide bowls rather than plates. It eats way neater that way and will be easier for the people at your table.

PREP: 10 minutes   *COOK:* 10 minutes

1× (16-ounce or 454g) jar of your favorite cooked—not fresh—**salsa** (I use salsa roja or roasted tomatillo salsa)

1 cup **chicken stock** or 1 cup hot water mixed with 1 teaspoon chicken bouillon paste

8 ounces (225g) **tortilla chips** (see Notes)

2 tablespoons **unsalted butter** or substitute vegetable oil

4 large **eggs**

Kosher salt and freshly ground **black pepper**

1 **avocado**, peeled, pitted, and cubed

2 **radishes**, thinly sliced

¼ cup coarsely chopped **cilantro leaves** and thin stems

½ cup crumbled **cotija** or feta cheese

NOTE   *The chips matter. Make sure you use true corn tortilla chips rather than masa flour chips (look on the label) which won't hold up as well to the cooking. Aside from that, choose from plain, yellow, round, or triangular chips. Dippers and blue corn versions tend to break up too much.*

1. In a large skillet, combine the salsa and stock. Bring to a gentle boil over medium heat. Reduce the heat to medium-low and simmer to reduce slightly, 3 to 5 minutes. Add the tortilla chips a handful at a time, gently stirring to combine. Continue until all the chips are added. Stir until the chips are completely coated.

2. In a large nonstick skillet over medium-high heat, melt the butter until sizzling (or heat the oil until shimmering), and swirl to fully coat the bottom. Crack the eggs into the skillet one at a time. Season with salt and pepper. Cover the skillet and cook until the whites are completely set and the yolks are just starting to thicken around the edges, 3 to 4 minutes. Remove the skillet from the heat.

3. To serve, divide the tortilla chips and sauce among the plates. Top each serving with one or two eggs. Generously garnish each with avocado, radish slices, cilantro, and cotija. Or place the toppings in small serving bowls and let everyone garnish their own.

MALAWACH

The recipe for this delicately flaky, buttery Yemenite flatbread was handed down to me by my grandmother on my father's side (Safta Rachel), and it proves the powerful idea of "breaking bread" with family, as it's ripped apart to serve. Bread can be such a fundamental staple and vehicle for other dishes that we often forget it can be an incredibly satisfying bite by itself. That's true of any homemade bread, but this one is in a league of its own. It's like a cross between puff pastry and a savory pancake. The dough freezes beautifully, ready to cook as needed. Malawach is a perfect partner for sides from savory to sweet and I give recommendations for each. Honestly, there's no bad way to eat it!

PREP: **10 minutes (plus 3½ hours resting time)**
COOK: **about 30 minutes**

FOR THE MALAWACH

3 cups *unbleached all-purpose flour*, plus more for dusting and rolling

2 teaspoons *kosher salt*

½ teaspoon *baking powder*

¼ cup *vegetable oil*, for resting

6 tablespoons *unsalted butter*, melted and cooled (or vegetable oil), for forming, plus unsalted butter or vegetable oil as needed for cooking

Tahina (see page 101), for serving

FOR THE SHAVED TOMATOES

1 to 2 large *plum tomatoes*

Flaky sea salt, such as Maldon

Extra virgin olive oil, for garnish

Very finely chopped *jalapeño*, for garnish (optional)

1. In a large mixing bowl, whisk together the flour, salt, and baking powder. Add 1¼ cups warm water and stir with a dough whisk or use your hands to work it to form a dough, adding more warm water, 1 tablespoon at a time, if the mixture is too dry. Shape the dough into a ball, cover with plastic wrap or a kitchen towel, and let the dough rest for 30 minutes.

2. Oil a baking sheet and pour about ¼ cup olive oil in a small bowl. Divide the dough into 6 equal pieces. Roll each piece between your hands into a ball, then dip it in the oil

to coat and transfer it to the baking sheet. Cover tightly with plastic wrap and let rest for at least 2 hours (the longer they rest, the easier they will be to shape).

3. Using your hands, gently stretch one ball at a time on a work surface into a rectangle approximately 8×12 inches (20×30cm). The dough should be paper thin; it's fine if it tears a little. Brush about 1 tablespoon melted butter or vegetable oil across the rectangle, leaving a ½-inch (12mm) border all around. Starting at one long side, roll the dough into a rope. Coil the rope around itself like a snail to make a flat circle. Place the circle under a towel. Repeat with the remaining dough balls.

4. Using a rolling pin, roll each "snail" between two sheets of parchment paper into an 8 to 9-inch (20 to 23cm) round. Stack the rounds, separated with sheets of parchment paper. Transfer the rounds to the freezer for at least 1 hour, or transfer to a tightly covered container and freeze for up to 3 months.

5. When you're ready to cook the malawach, grate the tomatoes on the coarse side of a box grater into a shallow bowl. Stir in a pinch or two of flaky sea salt. Set the shaved tomatoes aside until ready to serve. Just before serving, garnish with a drizzle of olive oil and some chopped jalapeño, if desired.

6. Preheat the oven to 200°F (100°C). Melt 1 tablespoon butter or heat vegetable oil in a medium cast-iron or nonstick skillet over medium heat. Carefully lay a malawach round in the pan and cook until the bread is golden brown on the bottom, about 2 minutes. Flip it and cook until it's golden brown on the other side, about

2 minutes more. (If the rounds have been frozen for an extended period, cook them for a bit longer.) Remove to a platter and keep warm in the oven. Repeat with the remaining rounds, adding more oil to the pan as needed.

7. Serve warm with the shaved tomato and tahina.

SWEET MALAWACH: For a sweet version, sprinkle the finished malawach with powdered sugar or drizzle with honey.

JACHNUN

I was introduced to jachnun basically in my infancy. It was just always around. It's truly a Jewish Yemenite delicacy and widely available in Israel, where it's sold in most corner markets and at lots of restaurants that serve breakfast. But most of the grandmas in Ramet Gan, the Dahari family base in Israel, make it at home. Beloved for Shabbat breakfast, it's in the same dough family as malawach, but jachnun is shaped into rolls and is a bit sweeter. You need a special jachnun pot (they're available on Amazon), and a good amount of time, because the dough is baked overnight low and slow to crispy, delicate perfection. The baking (and rolling) takes patience, but the result is worth the effort and time. This is a good "team effort" recipe to make with kids and friends. The rolls come out of the pot scintillatingly rich, with a deep golden-brown courtesy of a thin caramelized crust with a buttery, chewy interior. I strongly suggest you go all in and serve it with the traditional sides of Shabbat Eggs (see page 44 for a standalone recipe, or they can be cooked with the jachnun), Shaved Tomatoes (see page 52), and Schug (see page 104).

PREP: **1 hours and 20 minutes (plus 3 hours resting time)**
COOK: **11 to 12 hours**

¼ cup *granulated sugar*

2 tablespoons *date syrup* or honey

7 cups unbleached *all-purpose flour*

4 teaspoons *kosher salt*

½ teaspoon *baking powder*

½ cup *olive oil*, plus more for the work surface and your hands

About 14 tablespoons (7 ounces [198g]) *unsalted butter*, well softened, plus more for brushing the paper

8 large *eggs* (for Shabbat *egg*s)

Special Equipment: Stand mixer, jachnun pot

1. In the bowl of a stand mixer (or a large mixing bowl), whisk 2½ cups room temperature water, the sugar, and the date syrup to dissolve the sweeteners. Add the flour, salt, and baking powder. Attach the paddle attachment and mix on low until the dough forms. (Or stir the ingredients together in a large bowl.) With the dough hook, knead the dough (or knead by hand in the bowl) for 5 minutes. Cover the bowl with a clean kitchen towel and let the dough rest for 1 hour.

2. Knead the dough for 5 minutes, then cover the bowl with the kitchen towel and again let rest for 1 hour.

3. Oil a baking sheet and pour about ½ cup oil in a small bowl. Divide the dough into 12 equal pieces, dipping each in the oil to coat and transferring it to the baking sheet. Cover tightly with plastic wrap and let rest for at least 2 hours (the longer they rest, the easier they will be to shape).

4. Arrange an oven rack in the bottom of the oven and preheat the oven to 200°F (95°C). Cut 2 pieces of parchment to fit the bottom and top of a jachnun pan. Place one piece at the bottom of the pan and brush it with softened butter.

Recipe continues

5. Oil a work surface and your hands. Working with one dough ball at a time, use your hands to gently pat, pull, and stretch it into a rectangle roughly 12×18 inches (30cm×46cm). The dough should be thin and translucent; don't worry if it tears a little. Using your fingertips, gently smear a generous tablespoon of butter all over the dough. Starting at a long side, grasp the two corners and gently fold the dough over to the center. Grab the two corners of the opposite long side and fold them over the first fold, like a business letter to make a long, thin rectangle with three layers. Starting at one of the narrow ends, roll the rectangle into a cylinder. Lift the dough off the work surface and stretch it wider as you go, to keep the roll elongated and even.

6. Place the roll in the pan. Repeat with the remaining dough. Fill the bottom of the pan with one layer of rolls. Top with the remaining rolls, arranged at an angle to the first layer.

7. For Shabbat eggs, brush one side of the second parchment round with butter and place it buttered-side-down on top of the rolls. Gently arrange the eggs on top of the parchment around the edge of the pan.

8. Cover the pot with the lid. If the lid is not tight or you don't have a lid, wrap the whole pot tightly in aluminum foil. Bake until the jachnun is deep golden brown, 11 to 12 hours. Serve warm with the eggs, Shaved Tomatoes (see page 52), and Schug (see page 104).

KUBANEH
(Yemenite Slow-Cooked Bread)

My family always serves this bread with Yemenite Soup (see page 128), and it's as rich as brioche, with a deep brown exterior. Another Shabbat dish, it can be baked overnight in a very low oven, as with the Jachnun on page 55. It will be soft and tender inside with a golden, slightly crisp crust.

PREP: **45 minutes (plus 2 hours of resting times)**
COOK: **about 1 hour**

4 cups (560g) unbleached *all-purpose flour*, plus more as needed for kneading

1 tablespoon *sugar*

2 tablespoons *kosher salt*

2 teaspoons *instant yeast*

2 *large eggs*, divided

Vegetable oil, for handling the dough and the bowl

12 tablespoons (170g) *unsalted butter*, well softened, divided

Nigella seeds

Special Equipment: Stand mixer, Jachnun pot or 9-inch (23cm) springform pan

1. In the bowl of a stand mixer fitted with the dough hook (or a large mixing bowl), whisk together the flour, sugar, salt, and yeast.

2. Turn the mixer to low speed. Gradually add 1¼ cups warm water and 1 of the eggs (or stir into the dry ingredients in the bowl) and continue mixing until a soft, slightly sticky dough forms. If the dough is too dry, add a bit more water, 1 tablespoon at a time.

3. Increase the mixer to medium-low speed and knead until the dough is smooth and elastic, 7 to 8 minutes. (Or lightly flour the work surface. Turn the dough out of the mixing bowl and knead by hand for 8 to 10 minutes).

4. Add 4 tablespoons of the butter and continue kneading until the butter is completely incorporated and the dough is smooth, shiny, and elastic; it's fine if it's still a bit sticky.

5. Grease a large bowl with oil. With oiled hands, shape the dough into a ball, place it in the bowl, and turn to coat. Cover the bowl with a damp towel and let the dough rise in a warm place until it has doubled in size, about 1 hour.

6. When ready to shape the dough, generously grease a 9-inch (23cm) deep, round pan, such as a jachnun or a springform pan, with softened butter. Sprinkle some of the nigella seeds, if desired, over the bottom of the pan.

7. Generously oil a work surface. Deflate the dough and divide it into 6 equal portions. Working with one portion at a time, use your hands to gently pull and stretch it into a rectangle roughly 10×12 inches (25cm×30cm). The dough will be very thin; don't worry if it tears a little. Using your fingers, gently smear 1 rounded tablespoon of butter all over the dough. If desired, sprinkle some of the nigella seeds across the dough. Starting on a longer side, roll up the dough into a tight, long, thin cylinder. Beginning at one end, roll the cylinder into a tight coil. Place the coil upside down in the center of the prepared pan (so that the more uniform of the two sides is facing up).

8. Repeat with the remaining dough portions, butter, and most of the nigella seeds, if using, arranging the remaining coils very close together around the one in the center.

Recipe continues

9. Sprinkle the remaining nigella seeds, if desired, on top. Cover the pan with the damp kitchen towel or the jachnun pot lid and let the rolls rise in a warm place until they are puffy and almost fill the pan, about 1 hour.

10. Preheat the oven to 350°F (180°C). Whisk the remaining egg with 1 tablespoon water then gently brush the egg wash on top of the kubaneh. Place the springform or jachnun pan on a baking sheet in the oven. Bake for 40 minutes, then reduce the heat to 325°F (165°C) and continue to bake until golden brown on top and paler but fully cooked through between the coils, 20 to 25 minutes more.

11. Let the kubaneh cool in the pan for about 10 minutes. Turn out onto a wire rack and then flip them right-side-up on another wire rack or release and remove the springform side. Serve warm and invite diners to tear off the individual kubaneh with their hands.

Jake Cohen's
BAKLAVA BAKED OATMEAL

Everyone's fave Jew(ish) chef and my bestie, Jake Cohen, kindly shared this absolutely insane twist on oatmeal. Who would ever think to combine Baklava (which is a family recipe we've been making for generations, included in this book on page 218) with breakfast? Brilliant. It's also super healthy and satisfying. I have impressed many a brunch guest with this dish and it's so easy to whip up! I love you, Jakey!

<u>PREP:</u> **15 minutes**   <u>COOK:</u> **20 minutes**

2 cups *mixed nuts*, such as almonds, walnuts, and/or pistachios

½ cup *olive oil*, plus more for the baking dish

½ cup *honey*, plus more for serving

½ cup *plain low-fat Greek yogurt*

1 tablespoon *rose water*

1 teaspoon *ground cinnamon*

¾ teaspoon *kosher salt*

3 large *eggs*

2 cups (180g) *old-fashioned (rolled)* or *quick-cooking oats*

1 teaspoon *baking powder*

Fresh berries, for serving

Milk, *half-and-half*, or additional yogurt, for serving

1. Preheat the oven to 375°F (190°C). Oil a 9-inch (23cm) square baking dish.

2. In the bowl of a food processor, pulse the nuts until very finely chopped. (Or finely chop by hand with a large knife.)

3. In a large bowl, whisk together the olive oil, honey, yogurt, ½ cup water, rose water, cinnamon, salt, and eggs until smooth. Add in the chopped nuts, oats, and baking powder and mix until well incorporated. Spread evenly in the prepared baking dish.

4. Bake until set in the center and browning around the edges, about 20 minutes. Cut and transfer to cereal bowls, top with berries, drizzle with additional honey, and add milk, half-and-half, or yogurt. Serve warm.

EVERLASTING BRUNCH

The ultimate brunches seem to suspend time. They erase any
sense we have of the internal clock that pushes us through our everyday lives.
They're occasions that make you want to savor the people, food, and
drinks forever. Those brunches—rare, perfect moments that are so much more
than a meal—are what I call "everlasting." That's because, thanks to
the vivid happy memory, the brunch never really ends.

Want to make your own everlasting brunch? It's an easy art form that involves a little planning and a lot of understanding about how to make the occasion happen.

SOCIAL ZONES
Start with a strategy I use for any large party I host—social zones. Create comfortable, inviting areas around the room or rooms, enticing to cluster into small, intimate groups. These areas spur guests to talk, laugh, linger, and enjoy one another. Each gathering spot should flow into the next, so that guests naturally move between them and to and from the buffet.

MUSIC
As with all my get-togethers, I always have a soundtrack playing for brunch. I like something with a beat, but not as fast as I would use for a cocktail party. I set up a lengthy playlist or albums on shuffle, because "everlasting" is a long time. It's important to have music playing to greet guests. Music is an easy, warm welcome to any affair.

DRINKS
Start with a little social lubricant. Who doesn't love a splash of something intoxicating at a naughty hour? It's morning, so you have to have coffee. But it's brunch, so you have to have some adult beverages, too. I like to put a twist on the traditional brunch cocktails. I serve Bloody Marias (see page 194) and bellinis (peach puree and prosecco) instead of the traditional Bloody Marys and mimosas. That said, an everlasting brunch is all about options. I always put out fresh-squeezed juices to mix individual cocktails. That way, people can decide for themselves what they want to drink. I also open a bottle of light white wine and a light red like Barolo, or a chilled grenache.

TRANSITIONS
The everlasting brunch doesn't have courses; it has transitions. The dishes on the buffet table change seamlessly. There should never be an empty serving plate, because empty is a sign of an ending. That's why you need to have backups ready to go and a clear idea of what comes next. I prefer to start with the lighter stuff as appetite builders. I'll put out bowls of olives, fresh bagels, gravlax, quiche, and delicate crackers with airy spreads and dips.

Once people have settled in and are comfortable and mingling, I'll bring out heartier fare and anything heated, like a make-your-own Sabich platter (see page 42), Jachnun with Shabbat eggs (see page 44), and Chilaquiles (see page 51). After a drink and a snack, people are getting hungrier, so dishes like these hit the mark. People jump in, and that ensures the food gets eaten before it goes cold.

After everyone has had a chance to fill their plates, and have seconds if they want them, I'll remove the larger serving platters to make room for sweets and light finishing food. That should include a mix of textures and flavors, like Pistachio Cookies (see page 217) or Baklava (see page 218). I'll usually refill plates of seasonal fresh fruit, serve individual yogurt parfaits (like the Greek yogurt with Roasted Stone Fruit and Almonds on page 32), custard tartlets, almond cookies, rugelach, and babka from the local bakery. I'll add a couple savory items like a cheese platter or even chips and caviar. Whatever makes sense for grazing.

KEEP IT GOING
Everlasting means that the party isn't over so fast. Keep the coffee brewing and the glasses filled. Always have something to nibble on. Most of all, though, enjoy the company and hold tight to the forever memories you're making.

2

SUPPORTING

PLAYERS

When
PLANNING
A PARTY,

it's easy to concentrate on the main course and neglect the other parts of the menu. I try not to do that because I appreciate those supporting players! They are like the hilarious "minor" roles in a movie that you remember as much as the designated stars. Appetizers, side dishes, and condiments fall into this category.

Hors d'oeuvres, nibbles, snacks, munchies—they all warm the belly for what is to come afterward. Sometimes they *are* the party. It's fun to make a meal from a big spread of these easy-to-serve finger foods. The Quiche Tartlets (see page 147) and Egg Bites (see page 40) are both good bets because they're great served right out of the oven or at room temp. For something meaty, I might serve Kibbeh with a spicy Labneh as a dip (see pages 166 and 100). You can't go wrong with Hummus (see page 99) paired with bread, crackers, and fresh veggies. To brighten up the table and offer something on the light side, serve one of the salads in this chapter with small plates. Keep those platters filled! The only sin at a buffet is an empty dish.

I love a good cheese platter, but I avoid serving it alone to avoid the "Cheese-Gate" incident I had (IYKYK). Just serve your cheese as part of your spread, avoid your own cheese-gate, and give people the options they deserve!

When it comes to side dishes, my family loves carbs, especially rice, which in fact is almost exempt from the carb list. (I share a collection of our most-loved rice recipes in the next chapter.) Platanos and Tostones (see pages 86 and 88) are from Abe's Cuban heritage. We enjoy eggplant a lot, and I often make a pile of it to have on hand all week long. Brussels sprouts is a pretty versatile green vegetable and goes with so many different main courses, from chicken to steak.

Condiments are other "supporting players" that get a lot of love in my kitchen. Schug is an absolutely delicious, fresh medley that you can whip up so quickly and adds so much to any dish. Creating mayonnaise and ketchup from scratch is a fun and easy thing to do (see pages 92 and 93). You'd probably be surprised at how quickly they come together and also how much better they are than the store-bought versions. Garlicky Tahina sauce (see page 101) can be served with much more than just falafel. I personally like it mixed into my Israeli Salad (see page 74) as a dressing add-on.

Remember, it's the little things in life that make it interesting, and the same applies to the accompaniments to the main dishes on your menu. Also, it looks so cute and girly on a table if you have lots of colorful mini side dishes. These are the things that make me happy!

TARAMASALATA

This dip has origins in the eastern part of the Mediterrannean world—much like Abe, whose father was half Turkish and half Greek. (the name Lichy, has Turkish roots.) While most people serve it as a dip or mezze (I like to serve it with cucumber slices or chips), it's also good on scrambled eggs (FAVE), sliced tomatoes, and more. The classic version is made from salted mullet roe, but whitefish caviar is easier to find.

PREP: **15 minutes**

1¼ cups *panko*

1.75 ounces (50g) *whitefish roe* (caviar)

2 tablespoons grated *red onion* (grated using the large holes of a box grater)

3 tablespoons freshly squeezed *lemon juice* (from 1 to 2 lemons), as needed

6 tablespoons *extra virgin olive oil*, plus more for garnish

Kosher salt, to taste

Ground sumac, for garnish (optional)

Grated *lemon zest*, for garnish (optional)

Pita or other flatbread, sliced *cucumbers* or radishes, or *potato chips*, for serving

Special Equipment: Cheesecloth, food processor or blender

1. Place the panko in a medium mixing bowl and add enough water just to moisten (about 1 cup). Let stand for 3 minutes. Line a wire sieve with a double layer of cheesecloth. Scrape in the panko, then gather the edges of the cheesecloth and twist them together while you squeeze to extract as much liquid as possible from the panko.

2. Put the panko in the bowl of a food processor or the jar of a blender.

3. Set aside about ½ teaspoon of the roe for garnish, if desired. Add the remaining roe, onion, and lemon juice to the food processor or blender and pulse a few times to combine. Scrape down the sides of the bowl or jar.

4. With the machine running, gradually add the oil through the feed tube or lid opening in a very slow, steady stream. Scrape down the sides of the bowl or jar and season with salt (about ½ teaspoon). Process until fully combined and smooth, 30 to 60 seconds. Taste and season with additional salt and lemon juice as desired. The taramasalata can be refrigerated in a tightly sealed container for up to 5 days.

5. To serve, transfer the taramasalata to a small serving bowl. Garnish with the reserved roe, sumac, and lemon zest, if using. Serve with the pita, cucumbers, radishes, and/or potato chips for spreading and dipping.

ISRAELI SALAD

In our house, Israeli salad is served morning to night—with eggs for breakfast, in Sabich (see page 44) for lunch, and always as part of my Shabbat dinner spread. The main points to remember are that the vegetables must be cut into super small pieces, the salad should be cucumber heavy (don't use too much tomato) and be generous with the lemon. The smaller the cut of the veggies (almost like salsa), the better. Shepherd's salad is similar, but the vegetables tend to be cut larger. If you need to stretch it for a crowd, add a seeded and diced red bell pepper. You may find that you like it more that way anyway.

PREP: **20 minutes**   _COOK:_ **None**

6 *Persian cucumbers*, finely chopped

3 firm *plum tomatoes*, seeds mostly scraped out, finely chopped

1 small *red onion*, very finely chopped (about ¾ cup)

3 tablespoons finely chopped *flat-leaf parsley*

1 *red bell pepper*, seeded and finely chopped (optional)

4 tablespoons freshly squeezed *lemon juice*, or more as needed

¼ cup *extra-virgin olive oil*, plus more as needed

Flaky salt and freshly ground *black pepper*, to taste

1. In a large mixing bowl, combine the cucumbers, tomatoes, red onion, parsley, and bell pepper, if using.

2. Drizzle with 3 tablespoons lemon juice and the oil. Taste and add more lemon juice, if needed. Season generously with salt and pepper. Toss everything together until the salad is well coated. Season with additional salt, lemon juice, and oil, as desired. Let the salad stand at room temperature for about 10 minutes to allow the flavors to meld. The salad can be tightly covered and refrigerated for up to 4 days.

GREEK SALAD

This is a showstopper of a dish—so beautiful! Unlike the Israeli Salad (see page 75), the vegetables for a Greek Salad should be chunky. Keep the feta in a big block and let the guests dig into the cheese for the amount they want. You know how I like interactive food! Sometimes I garnish the salad with lemon wedges so each person can add as much as they like. This is a chance to use a very good, imported feta packed in brine from a cheese shop.

PREP: 20 minutes (including resting time)   *COOK:* None

4 ripe *plum tomatoes*

6 *Persian cucumbers*

1 *green bell pepper*, seeded and cut into 2-inch (2.5cm) pieces

1 small *red onion*, chopped into 2-inch (2.5cm) pieces

1 cup drained unpitted or pitted *Kalamata olives*

3 tablespoons *extra virgin olive oil*, as needed

2 tablespoon freshly squeezed *lemon juice*, or to taste

Kosher salt and freshly ground *black pepper*, to taste

7 ounces (200g) block *sheep's milk feta*, plus 1 to 2 tablespoons of its brine

2 teaspoons *dried oregano*, preferably Greek if you have it

1. Cut the tomatoes lengthwise into 6 wedges, then slice each wedge in half, or in thirds if the tomatoes are very large. Transfer to a large serving bowl.

2. Peel the cucumber lengthwise at intervals so that it is striped. Cut into 2-inch (2.5cm) pieces and add to the bowl with the green pepper, red onion, and olives.

3. Drizzle with the feta brine, oil, and lemon juice. Season with the salt and pepper and toss to coat and mix.

4. Place the full block of feta on top of the salad. Sprinkle with the oregano and a little more salt and pepper. Be careful not to add too much salt, since the feta and olives are already quite salty. Drizzle with additional oil and lemon juice.

5. Let stand at room temperature for about 20 minutes before serving to allow the flavors to meld. The leftover salad can be stored in an airtight container and refrigerated for up to 4 days.

Shredded CABBAGE SALAD

I always make a lot of this salad with an entire cabbage because otherwise the other half just sits in my fridge forever. If I have too much remaining at the end of a party that's fine because it lasts for over a week and literally just keeps getting better as it marinates. You can keep adding things to it for different lunch meals like nuts, grilled chicken, tuna, etc.

PREP: **3 hours and 15 minutes (including chilling time)**
COOK: **None**

1 small (2lb, 955g) head *red cabbage*

¾ cup *mayonnaise*

2 tablespoons freshly squeezed *lemon juice*

1½ tablespoon *red wine vinegar*

1 teaspoon *kosher salt*

½ teaspoon freshly ground *black pepper*

1 bunch *flat-leaf parsley*, leaves and tender stems
    coarsely chopped, plus more for garnish

Special Equipment: Mandoline

1. Cut the cabbage through the core into 4 wedges. Cut out and discard the core. Using a mandoline or large, sharp knife, shred the cabbage. (You should have about 10 cups). Place it in a large mixing bowl.

2. In a small mixing bowl, whisk the mayonnaise, lemon juice, vinegar, salt, and pepper.

3. Pour about half of the dressing over the cabbage, add the chopped parsley, and toss to coat. Add more dressing if the salad seems dry. Season with additional salt and pepper. Cover the salad and dressing separately with plastic wrap. Refrigerate at least 3 hours before serving for the salad flavors to meld.

4. Before serving, toss with as much additional dressing as desired, season again to taste with salt and pepper, and sprinkle with the parsley. Leftover salad can be covered and refrigerated for up to 2 weeks.

MOROCCAN CIGARS

Crispy and spicy hors d'oeuvres like these Moroccan cigars are always a crowd pleaser, so I tend to make a lot. The spices tease the appetite, and there's something about the crunch of the phyllo that keeps you coming back for more. These are especially fun to make with a couple of extra helping hands.

PREP: **40 minutes (including cooling time)**
COOK: **30 minutes**

1 tablespoon *extra-virgin olive oil*

1 small *yellow onion*, finely chopped (about 1 cup)

2 *garlic cloves*, minced

1¾ teaspoon *kosher salt*, divided

1 pound (450g) *ground beef* or lamb

1 teaspoon *ground cumin*

½ teaspoon *ground cinnamon*

½ teaspoon *ground sweet paprika*

¼ teaspoon *ground ginger*

¼ teaspoon *ground turmeric*

¼ teaspoon freshly ground *black pepper*

¼ cup finely chopped *flat-leaf parsley* leaves and tender stems

¼ cup finely chopped *cilantro leaves* and tender stems

¼ cup *pine nuts* or slivered almonds, toasted (optional or almonds coarsely chopped)

2 tablespoons *golden raisins* (optional)

1 large *egg* beaten with 1 tbsp water, for egg wash and sealing

About ten 13×18-inch (33×46cm) *phyllo sheets* (about ½ of a 1lb [450g] package)

Vegetable oil, for frying

Green or *Red Schug* (see page 104) and *Labneh* (see page 100), for serving

1. In a large skillet, heat the olive oil over medium heat. Add the onion, garlic, and ¼ teaspoon salt. Cook, stirring occasionally, until soft and translucent, about 7 minutes. Add the ground beef and 1½ teaspoons salt, the cumin, cinnamon, paprika, ginger, turmeric, and a few grindings of pepper. Cook, stirring and breaking up the meat with the side of the spoon, until browned, about 8 minutes. Stir in the parsley, cilantro, pine nuts, and raisins, if using. Remove from the heat and let the filling cool.

2. Have ready a large baking sheet or platter and two clean, damp kitchen towels. Cut the phyllo sheets into thirds crosswise to get 30 rectangles about 6×13 inches (15×33cm) each. Stack them together on your work surface and cover with a damp towel to keep them from drying out.

3. Working with 1 filo rectangle at a time, put 1 tablespoon of the filling across one short end about ½ inch (12mm) from the bottom edge. Roll up tightly like a cigar, folding in the long sides as you go to enclose the filling. Brush the end with a bit of egg wash and seal the rolls. Transfer the rolled cigar to the baking sheet, seam-side down, with the other towel. Repeat with the remaining phyllo and filling. Line another baking sheet with paper towels and set it next to the stovetop.

4. Pour enough vegetable oil in a large deep skillet to come about ½ inch (12mm) up the sides. Heat over medium heat until the oil is hot and shimmering but not smoking (or 350°F (180°C) on an instant-read thermometer).

5. In batches, without crowding, add the cigars to the skillet and fry, turning often with tongs, until crisp and golden brown, about 3 minutes total, adjusting the heat as need to keep the oil temperature steady. Transfer to paper towels to drain. Continue with the remaining cigars, adding more oil to the pan if necessary.

6. Serve hot, with bowls of Schug (see page 104) and Labneh (see page 100), for dipping.

LACHUCH
(Yemenite Pancakes)

If you've ever been to an Ethiopian restaurant, you've had a spongy teff flour flatbread named injera. Its Yemenite cousin, made from wheat, is similar. Note that unlike other pan-cooked breads, this is not flipped over. You can serve them with Labneh (see page 100) and a sprinkle of za'atar on top and pair it with meatballs, chicken and potatoes, soup—really anything. They are light, airy, and delish.

PREP: **1 hour and 15 minutes (including fermentation time)** *COOK:* **25 minutes**

4 cups unbleached ***all-purpose flour***

2 teaspoons ***instant yeast***

2 teaspoons ***baking powder***

1 tablespoon ***sugar***

2 teaspoons ***kosher salt***

Vegetable oil, for cooking

1. In a large mixing bowl, whisk the flour, yeast, baking powder, sugar, and salt. Whisk in 3½ cups warm tap water, whisking to make a smooth, lump-free batter. It should be thick, but pourable, like pancake batter. Add up to another ½ cup warm water if necessary.

2. Cover the bowl with plastic wrap or a moistened kitchen towel and let it stand in a warm spot for 1 hour. Stir in the baking powder and let stand until it becomes bubbly and rises a little bit.

3. Lightly grease a 12-inch (30.5cm) nonstick skillet. Stir the batter gently and ladle about ½ cup into the center of the pan. Spread it out slightly with the back of the ladle to form a thin circle that fills the bottom of the pan.

4. Place the pan over medium-low heat and cook until the surface is covered with bubbles, looks dry, with a lightly colored bottom, and the edges start to lift slightly, 2 to 3 minutes. Transfer the lachuch to a large plate or platter.

5. Carefully run the bottom of the upside-down pan under cold running water until it is completely cooled. Dry the pan thoroughly. Return it to the heat and repeat the steps above until all the batter is used, stacking the lachuch on top of each other on the platter. Serve warm.

KITCHRI
(Iraqi Lentils and Rice with Caramelized Onions)

This dish of rice and lentils with a topping of caramelized onions is the perfect mix of sweet and savory. You can serve it as a side dish or as the main event for a simple lunch/dinner, as thin lentils cook more quickly than other legumes. I suppose you can make this with standard brown lentils, but the red ones are much more attractive and tend to be creamier. If your supermarket doesn't carry them, you can find them at Indian grocers. My kids really love to eat this with Labneh (see page 100). It's one of Layla's faves (sans the onion).

PREP: 20 minutes   COOK: 50 minutes to 1 hour
TOTAL: 1 hour and 20 minutes

FOR THE KITCHRI

3 tablespoons *extra virgin olive oil*

1 large **onion**, chopped

4 **cloves garlic**, finely chopped

¼ cup **tomato paste**

1 tablespoon **ground cumin**

2 cups **basmati rice**, well rinsed

1 cup **red lentils,** rinsed and sorted over for stones

1× 15 ounce (425g) can of **tomato sauce**

1 tablespoon **kosher salt**

½ teaspoon freshly ground **black pepper**

Labneh (see page 100), for serving

FOR THE ONION TOPPING

¼ cup **extra virgin olive oil**

2 large **onions**, thinly sliced

2 teaspoons **kosher salt**

1. Heat the oil in a Dutch oven or large saucepan over medium heat. Add the onion and cook, stirring, until softened, about 8 minutes. Stir in the garlic and cook until the onion is golden, about 2 minutes more. Stir in the tomato paste and cumin and cook until fragrant and the paste deepens in color, about 1 minute. Add the rice and lentils to the pot and mix well. Stir in 5½ cups water with the tomato sauce, salt, and pepper.

2. Bring to a boil. Reduce the heat to low, cover, and simmer until the rice and lentils are tender and the liquid is absorbed, 20 to 25 minutes. Let stand, covered, for 5 minutes.

3. Meanwhile, to make the topping: Heat the oil in a skillet over medium heat. Add the onion and salt and cook, stirring occasionally, until the onions are golden brown and caramelized, 20 to 25 minutes.

4. Fluff the rice and lentils with a fork and transfer to a serving dish. Top with the caramelized onions or serve, with the Labneh (see page 100), on the side.

PLATANOS
(Cuban Fried Plantains)

Fried plantains are a staple in Cuban cuisine, and Abe's mom (Regla) is an expert at cooking them. She advises that the plantains should be ripe with some black spots, but not blackened and soft. They may remind you of a banana, but starchier and more suited to spicy dishes. When I first met Abe's family and walked in the door for Shabbat dinner, Abe looked at me and said, my mom made Platanos, that means someone special is coming to dinner. This is a simple, delicious dish that holds a special place.

PREP: **5 minutes**   *COOK:* **10 to 15 minutes**

2 large, ripe **plantains**
Vegetable oil, for frying
Kosher salt

1. To peel the plantains, trim off both ends. Using a paring knife, cut lengthwise along the ridges through the skin and just to the flesh. Peel off and discard the skin in sections. Cut the plantains on the diagonal into slices about ½-inch (12mm) thick.

2. Line a baking sheet with paper towels and set it next to the stovetop.

3. Preheat the oven to 200°F (95°C). Pour enough vegetable oil to come about ¼ inch (3mm) up the sides of a large, deep skillet. Heat over medium-high heat until the oil is shimmering, but not smoking, or it reaches 350°F (180°C) on an instant-read thermometer.

4. In batches, without crowding, add the plantains to the skillet. Fry, flipping about halfway during cooking, until golden brown, about 2 minutes per side. Using a slotted spoon, transfer to the paper towels and sprinkle lightly with salt. Keep warm in the oven. Repeat with the remaining plantains, adding more oil to the pan if necessary. (Be sure to heat the extra oil before adding more plantains.) Serve warm.

TOSTONES
(Twice-Fried Plantains with Lime-Garlic Mojo)

These are the flip side of the Platanos (see page 87) because the plantains for these are made with green, firm, "unripe" plantains. While the mojo is optional, it does brighten up the starchiness. They go with Picadillo (see page 137), shredded chicken, honestly ANYTHING. I love these so much.

PREP: **8 minutes**   *COOK:* **15 to 20 minutes**

FOR THE MOJO
¼ cup (60ml) *extra virgin olive oil*

3 tablespoons freshly squeezed *lime juice*

3 *garlic cloves*, minced

2 tablespoons chopped *flat-leaf parsley* leaves and tender stems

½ teaspoon *kosher salt*

FOR THE TOSTONES
2 large *green plantains*

Vegetable oil, for frying

Kosher salt

1. To make the mojo, in a small bowl, stir the olive oil, lime juice, garlic, parsley, and salt. Set aside.

2. To peel the plantains, cut off both ends. Using a paring knife, cut lengthwise along the ridges through the skin and just to the flesh. Peel off and discard the skin in sections. Cut the plantains on the diagonal into slices about ½-inch (12mm) thick. Cut the plantains into 1-inch (2.5cm) thick slices.

3. Preheat the oven to 200°F (95°C). Line a baking sheet with paper towels and set it next to the stovetop. Pour enough vegetable oil to come about ½ inch (6mm) up the sides of a large, deep skillet. Heat over medium-high heat until the oil is shimmering, but not smoking, or it reaches 350°F (180°C) on an instant-read thermometer.

4. In batches, without crowding, add the plantains to the skillet. Fry, flipping about halfway during cooking, until beginning to brown, about 2 ½ minutes per side. Using a slotted spoon, transfer to the paper towels. Keep warm in the oven. Repeat with the remaining plantains, adding more oil to the pan if necessary. (Be sure to heat the extra oil before adding more plantains.)

5. Using the bottom of a flat glass or bowl, gently press each plantain slice to about ¼-inch (3mm) thick; try not to break them.

6. Line another baking sheet with fresh paper towels. In batches, return the flattened plantains to the hot oil in a single layer. Fry, flipping about halfway during cooking, until crispy and golden brown, about 2½ minutes per side. Using the slotted spoon, transfer to the paper towels. Lightly sprinkle with salt. Continue with the remaining plantains, reheating the oil as needed.

7. Serve warm, with the mojo on the side.

Zesty Roasted
POTATO WEDGES

Roasted potato wedges are one of the easiest and most popular of all sides, and I'm a girl who loves her potatoes. But even such a simple dish has a few tricks that I've learned, and I'm going to share. A great tip is to soak the wedges in cold water to remove extra starch so they bake up nice and crisp. A flavorful seasoning doesn't hurt, either. I like to serve these as finger food—dip away!

PREP: **25 to 35 minutes (including soaking time)**
COOK: **35 to 40 minutes**

4 large *russet potatoes*, scrubbed but unpeeled

3 tablespoons *extra virgin olive oil*

1½ teaspoons *garlic powder*

1 teaspoon *onion powder*

1 teaspoon *smoked paprika*

1 teaspoon crushed *dried rosemary*

1 teaspoon *kosher salt*

½ teaspoon freshly ground *black pepper*

⅛ teaspoon *cayenne pepper*

2 tablespoons freshly grated *Parmesan cheese*

Chopped *fresh parsley* leaves and tender stems, for garnish

Flaky salt, for garnish

Homemade Ketchup (see page 92), *Homemade Mayonnaise* (see page 93), or your favorite dipping sauces, for serving

1. Preheat the oven to 425°F (220°C) and line 2 large baking sheets with parchment paper. Cut each potato lengthwise into 8 wedges.

2. While the oven is preheating, soak the wedges in cold water to cover for 20 to 30 minutes. Drain and pat the wedges completely dry with a clean towel. Transfer to a large bowl. Add the oil, garlic powder, onion powder, smoked paprika, rosemary, salt, pepper, and cayenne, and toss. Add the Parmesan and toss again. Arrange the wedges, flat-side down, on the baking sheets, leaving a little space between them.

3. Bake, flipping the potatoes over halfway through cooking, until they are golden and crispy on the outside and tender inside, 35 to 40 minutes.

4. Sprinkle with the parsley, a bit of flaky salt, and serve hot, with the dipping sauce(s) of your choice.

Simple Homemade
KETCHUP

Instead of overly sweet and gloppy bottled ketchup made with tons of preservatives and hidden sweeteners, I make this super-simple ketchup for my family. I can control the sweet-tangy balance that we all like. Just be careful not to use too much sugar or vinegar and taste freely as you go along.

PREP: **10 minutes**   *COOK:* **None**   *TOTAL:* **10 minutes**

2× 6-ounce (170g) cans of **tomato paste**

3 tablespoons **distilled white** or **apple cider vinegar**, plus more as needed

1½ tablespoons **sugar**, plus more as needed

¼ teaspoon **kosher salt**, plus more as needed

Pinch of **onion powder** (optional)

Pinch of **allspice** (optional)

Special Equipment: Blender

1. In the jar of a blender, process the tomato paste, vinegar, sugar, salt, onion powder, if using, allspice, if using, and ¼ cup water until smooth. (Alternatively, you may whisk them together in a medium bowl.) If the mixture seems thick, slowly whisk in water, 1 tablespoon at a time, to reach the desired consistency.

2. Taste and add more vinegar, sugar, or salt as needed.

3. Transfer the ketchup to an airtight container and refrigerate for at least 30 minutes to allow the flavors to meld. (The ketchup can be refrigerated for up to 3 weeks.)

MAKES
ABOUT
2½
cups

Homemade MAYO

This is another condiment that may be easy to buy but is almost equally easy to make. A food processor will give you creamy, delicious mayonnaise in a minute or two, but people have been making it by hand for centuries. Two big tips: Be sure the eggs are at room temp and only use a splash of EVOO at the end for a little olive flavor. If you use all olive oil, the mayo will separate. I also prefer white pepper to black for this. Make it once, and you'll be converted, as I was. The recipe is easy to cut in half.

PREP: 10 to 15 minutes   *COOK:* None

2 large *eggs*, at room temperature (see Note)

2 tablespoons *Dijon mustard*

2 tablespoons *white wine vinegar*, freshly squeezed *lemon juice*, or a combination, as needed

2 cups neutral *vegetable oil*, such as canola, avocado, or grapeseed

2 tablespoons *extra virgin olive oil* (optional)

Kosher salt and freshly ground *white or black pepper*

Special Equipment: Food processor

1. Pulse the eggs, Dijon mustard, vinegar and/or lemon juice, and a pinch of salt in a food processor until combined. (Or whisk in a medium bowl.)

2. With the food processor running, pour in the neutral oil through the feed tube to emulsify the mayonnaise. This will take about 2 minutes—don't rush it. As it begins to thicken, you can increase the flow of the oil slightly. Add the olive oil, if using, and pulse to combine. (Or, for the low-tech option, put the bowl on a folded wet kitchen towel to stabilize it. Whisking constantly, dribble in the neutral oil very slowly, then whisk in the olive oil.) Season with salt, white pepper, and more vinegar, as needed.

3. Store in a tightly covered container in the refrigerator for up to 1 week.

NOTE   *The eggs must be at room temperature, not refrigerator-cold for the mayonnaise to emulsify. To quickly warm the eggs, put the unshelled eggs in a bowl of hot tap water, cover, and let stand for 5 minutes to lose their chill. That's it, and it works any time you need room-temp eggs.*

VARIATIONS

HERB MAYONNAISE: Add ½ cup finely chopped mixed fresh herbs, such as parsley, chives, tarragon, and dill, in any combination, to the mayonnaise and pulse to combine. Add salt and lemon juice to taste.

SPICY MAYONNAISE: Add 2 tablespoons Green or Red Schug (see page 104) into the mayonnaise and pulse to combine. Add salt and lemon juice to taste.

Fried EGGPLANT THINS

A well-stocked fridge makes me happy. One of the best things I can find stashed away for quick meals is a pile of eggplant. I use it often for Sabich (page 42), but it's a lifesaver when you think you don't have anything to make into lunch or dinner since it can be added to many different dishes. Lots of times I'll have a slice of buttered toast, fried eggplant, and a hardboiled egg when I need a quick snack.

PREP: **40 minutes (including draining time)**
COOK: **20 minutes**

3 small ***eggplant*** (about 1½ pounds total), sliced lengthwise ⅛-inch (3mm) thick

2 teaspoons ***kosher salt***

Vegetable oil, for frying

Special Equipment: Instant-read thermometer

1. Line 2 baking sheets with paper towels. Use a sharp knife to very thinly slice the eggplant lengthwise. Place the eggplant slices on the baking sheets; it's okay if the slices overlap a bit, but don't pile them on top of each other. Sprinkle with salt. Let the eggplant stand to draw out excess moisture and bitterness, about 30 minutes or longer. Pat the eggplant dry with paper towels. Line one of the baking sheets with fresh paper towels and place it next to the stovetop.

2. Pour enough oil to come about ¼ inch (6mm) up the sides of a large, deep skillet. Heat over medium-high heat until the oil is shimmering, but not smoking, or reaches 350°F (180°C) on an instant-read thermometer.

3. In batches, without crowding, add the eggplant in a single layer, but they can overlap slightly. Fry, flipping halfway through cooking, until golden on both sides, 3 to 4 minutes total. Reduce the heat if the oil begins to smoke. Use tongs or a slotted spatula to transfer the eggplant to the paper towels. Repeat with the remaining eggplant slices, adding more oil to the pan as needed. Serve warm or cool. (The eggplant can be cooled and refrigerated in a tightly covered container for up to 4 days.)

CRISPY
BRUSSELS SPROUTS
with Honey and Lime

In the Dark Ages of kitchen history, Brussels sprouts were always boiled. Now, in these enlightened days, you find them roasted to tenderness. I give them a light dressing of lime and honey to contrast with their cabbage-y side.

PREP: **5 minutes**   *COOK:* **20 minutes**

2 pounds (900g) **Brussels sprouts**, trimmed and halved

3 tablespoons *extra-virgin olive oil*

2 teaspoons *kosher salt*

1 teaspoon freshly ground **black pepper**

2 tablespoons freshly squeezed **lime juice**

1 tablespoon **honey**

¼ teaspoon **crushed hot red pepper**, or to taste (optional)

1. Preheat the oven to 425°F (220°C). Line 2 baking sheets with parchment paper.

2. In a large bowl, toss the halved Brussels sprouts with the oil, salt, and pepper to coat. Spread, flat side down, on the baking sheets, spreading them out so they are not touching.

3. Roast until tender when pierced with a sharp knife and the edges are browned and crispy, about 20 minutes.

4. Meanwhile, in a small bowl, whisk the lime juice, honey, and crushed red pepper, if using. Transfer the Brussels sprouts to a large bowl. Drizzle with the lime mixture and toss to coat. Serve warm.

SECRET
Ingredients
No More

The Israeli kitchen is a fragrant place, and it's the spice blends that are often responsible for the aroma. These mixes are becoming easier to purchase, but it's fun to make your own. The same can be said for labneh. These are simple, straightforward recipes. Store the Hawaji and Baharat in airtight jars in a cool, dark place for up to 6 months, or freeze for up to 1 year.

HAWAIJ   In a small bowl, combine 2 tablespoons each of ground cumin, freshly ground black pepper, and ground turmeric. Add 2 teaspoons ground cardamom and, if you wish, 1 teaspoon ground cloves. Mix until uniform in color. Makes 7 tablespoons of spice blend.

BAHARAT   In a small bowl combine 1 tablespoon each freshly ground black pepper, ground cumin, ground coriander, and paprika, along with ½ tablespoon each ground cinnamon, ground cloves, ground cardamom, and ground nutmeg. Makes 6 tablespoons of spice blend.

ZA'ATAR   In a small bowl, mix 2 tablespoons dried oregano, 1 tablespoon each dried marjoram and sesame seeds, 1 teaspoon ground sumac, and ½ teaspoon Aleppo pepper. Mix until uniform in color. Makes 4½ tablespoons of spice blend.

HUMMUS

Hummus is one of the most versatile "sauces" in the Israeli kitchen. Sure, it's a dip to serve with pita. But if you need a quick accompaniment for a piece of fish, chicken, or even french fries, reach for the hummus. Need an afternoon snack? Put out the hummus and carrots or a piece of bread. I always keep a can of garbanzo beans and my homemade (thin) tahini in the house, so I am never without my hummus. I've found that a combination of thin tahini (and a bit of the bean liquid, aka aquafaba) gives the hummus the lightest texture.

PREP: **15 minutes**   *COOK:* **None**   *TOTAL:* **15 minutes**

1× 15.5 ounces (439g) ***can of chickpeas***, drained over a bowl, and rinsed (about 1½ cups)

½ cup ***Tahini*** (see page 101)

¼ cup freshly squeezed ***lemon juice*** (from 1 to 2 lemons), plus more as needed

3 ***garlic cloves***, finely minced or grated

1 teaspoon ***ground cumin*** (optional)

1 teaspoon ***kosher salt***, or to taste

2 tablespoons ***extra virgin olive oil***, plus more for drizzling

Sweet paprika or ground sumac, for garnish

Pita bread, cut into wedges, or assorted fresh vegetables, for serving

Special Equipment: Food processor or blender

1. In the bowl of a food processor or jar of a blender, process the garbanzo beans into a rough paste, scraping down the sides as needed.

2. Add the tahini, lemon juice, garlic, cumin, and salt. Process until smooth and creamy, about 2 minutes. With the machine running, drizzle in the oil through the feed tube or lid opening. Then slowly drizzle in the reserved liquid from the can of chickpeas or cold water, 1 tablespoon at a time, scraping down the sides of the bowl or jar once or twice. Season with additional lemon juice and salt, as needed, and pulse to mix. Transfer to an airtight container for storage or serve immediately. (The hummus can be refrigerated for up to 4 days.)

3. To serve the hummus, transfer to a serving bowl. Drizzle with more olive oil and sprinkle with paprika or sumac and serve with the pita or vegetables.

LABNEH

Thick and creamy labneh is what yogurt wants to be when it grows up. And when I was growing up, it was served with everything. We had it with lentils, rice, eggs, you name it. Drain off the whey from your favorite Greek yogurt, and you get a glorious glob of tangy goodness that can be served plain as a condiment, transformed into a dip, or used as a spread. Make it with full-fat yogurt if you want it to taste the way it should, but if you're looking for something lighter, low-fat is fine, too (I guess).

PREP: **12 to 14 hours (including straining)** *COOK:* **None**
TOTAL: **12 to 14 hours**

2 cups *whole milk* (not low- or nonfat) *plain Greek yogurt*

½ teaspoon *kosher salt*

Za'atar (see page 98)

¼ teaspoon freshly squeezed *lemon juice*

Extra virgin olive oil, for drizzling

Finely chopped *fresh herbs*, such as mint or thyme, za'atar, or sumac, for serving

Special Equipment: Wire sieve, cheesecloth

1. In a medium mixing bowl, stir the yogurt and salt together. Line a wire sieve with a double layer of cheesecloth or a cut-open coffee filter and suspend it over a tall bowl. Pour in the salted yogurt, then gather the edges of the cheesecloth to cover the yogurt (or cover it with a second cut-open filter).

2. Refrigerate the entire setup so that it can drain for 12 to 24 hours; the liquid whey will collect in the bowl. The longer the labneh drains, the thicker it will become. Pour out the whey as it collects, if you wish, reserving it for another use, such as soup.

3. Transfer the drained labneh to an airtight container. The labneh can be refrigerated for up to 1 week. To serve, spoon the labneh into a serving bowl, drizzle with olive oil, and sprinkle with your preferred herbs and/or spices.

TAHINA SAUCE

What comes first, the tahini or the tahina? The answer is the tahini, which is an all-purpose sesame seed paste (mine is on the thin side, not the thick stuff you get at the supermarket). That, in turn, is used to make a smooth sauce named tahina, the perfect condiment to so many Middle Eastern sandwiches, and an essential ingredient in hummus.

PREP: **15 minutes**   COOK: **5 minutes, plus cooling time for the seeds**   TOTAL: **20 minutes**

TAHINI PUREE

1 cup hulled or unhulled *sesame seeds*

3 tablespoons neutral-flavored *vegetable oil*, such as avocado or grapeseed

Pinch of *kosher salt*

TAHINA SAUCE

½ cup *Tahini* (see above) or use store-bought tahini

¼ cup freshly squeezed *lemon juice*

3 *garlic cloves*, finely minced or grated

1 teaspoon *kosher salt*

⅛ teaspoon *ground cumin* (optional)

Fresh *flat-leaf parsley* leaves and tender stems, chopped (for garnish)

Special Equipment: Food processor or blender

1. To make the tahini, in a dry skillet over medium heat, lightly toast the sesame seeds, stirring often, until they are fragrant and just begin to turn golden, about 3 minutes. They can burn in a flash so stir and watch them carefully. Immediately transfer the seeds to a plate and let cool. (If you leave them in the pan, they may burn, even off the heat.)

2. Transfer the sesame seeds to the bowl of a food processor or the jar of a blender and process until they begin to break down. With the machine running, gradually drizzle in the oil. Process, scraping down the sides of the bowl or jar as needed, until the consistency is smooth and creamy. To thin the tahini to the pourable consistency that I prefer, or to whatever consistency you like, add water 1 teaspoon at a time, blending after each addition. Add a pinch of salt, and blend again. Transfer to an airtight container. (The tahini can be refrigerated for up to 1 month.) Makes about ⅔ cup tahini puree.

3. To make the tahina sauce, in a medium mixing bowl, whisk together the tahini, lemon juice, garlic, salt, and cumin, if using. It's normal for the mixture to thicken. Gradually whisk in cold water, 1 tablespoon at a time, until the tahina reaches your desired consistency. Season with more lemon juice and salt, or even another garlic clove. Transfer to an airtight container. The tahina can be refrigerated for up to 1 week. Sprinkle with parsley before serving, if desired.

Homemade BUTTER

Put this with my other "fun stuff to make at home that is better than the store-bought versions." Spread this on your bagel or toast, and you will wonder where it's been all your life. For a real farmhouse taste (I mean that in the best way), use an organic brand of cream that has not been ultra-pasteurized. A local dairy or farmers market might carry it. A little salt brings out the flavor and acts as a preservative, but honestly, this butter is all about freshness anyway.

PREP: **1 hour and 15 minutes (including chill time)**
COOK: **None** *TOTAL:* **1 hour and 15 minutes**

2 cups **heavy cream**, preferably pasteurized (but not ultra-pasteurized)

¼ teaspoon **kosher salt**

Special Equipment: Stand mixer with the paddle attachment, wire sieve, cheesecloth

1. Pour the heavy cream into the bowl of a stand mixer fitted with the paddle attachment. Drape a large kitchen towel over the mixer to contain the splashing. On low speed, beat the cream. As the cream thickens, gradually increase the speed to medium-high. At first, you will have whipped cream and then it will look curdled after 3 to 5 minutes. Keep beating until the mixture has fully separated into a thick yellow mass of butter in liquid.

2. Line a wire sieve set over a tall bowl with a double layer of cheesecloth. Pour the butter mixture into the sieve and let the liquid drain into the bowl. Reserve the drained liquid for another use (see Note). Gather up the cheesecloth and twist to wring out excess liquid from the butter. Working under a stream of cold water, knead the butter to remove more liquid. (In spite of the running water, you will feel the butter get firmer.)

3. Transfer to a small bowl, add the salt, and knead into the butter. For the nicest presentation, cut an 8-inch (20cm) sheet of parchment or waxed paper. Spoon the butter into a log in the center of the paper. Roll to wrap the butter. Twist the paper at both ends in opposite directions to shape and tighten the roll. Or place the mass of butter in an airtight container. Refrigerate for at least 1 hour to firm and chill for up to 1 week. The butter can also be frozen for up to 6 months and thawed before using.

NOTE *The drained liquid is old-fashioned buttermilk, but it isn't cultured and acidic like the modern supermarket version. Today's (mostly baking) recipes use thick, clabbered buttermilk. If you want to simulate commercial buttermilk, stir 2 teaspoons white distilled or apple cider vinegar into each ½ cup of the butter-liquid.*

VARIATIONS

GARLIC-CILANTRO BUTTER: In a small mixing bowl, using a silicone spatula, mash the butter with 3 minced garlic cloves and 1½ tablespoons finely chopped cilantro until combined. Wrap and store as above.

SMOKY CHILE BUTTER: In a small mixing bowl using a silicone spatula, mash the butter with 1 tablespoon seeded and minced fresh chiles (such as Fresno, serrano, or green or red jalapeño) and ¼ teaspoon smoked paprika until combined. Wrap and store as above.

GREEN SCHUG
(Yemenite Hot Sauce)

Schug used to be a kind of secret sauce that only Yemenites and Israelis knew about. Lately, it's branched out and become many a chef's favorite condiment. Of course, with my heritage, it's been a standard in our family kitchen for years. Add to soups or stews, spread on sandwiches, mix into stuffed egg fillings, stir into mayonnaise—in other words, treat it like any other hot sauce, but so much more fresh!

PREP: **15 minutes**   *COOK:* **None**   *TOTAL:* **15 minutes**

1 pound (450g) *fresh green chiles*, such as serrano or jalapeño (10 to 12 chilies)

4 *garlic cloves*, coarsely chopped

1 teaspoon *ground cumin*

1 teaspoon *ground coriander*

½ teaspoon *ground cardamom*

1 teaspoon *kosher salt*, or to taste

1 cup coarsely chopped *fresh cilantro leaves* and tender stems

¼ cup coarsely chopped *flat leaf parsley* leaves and tender stems, coarsely chopped

2 tablespoons freshly squeezed *lemon juice*, plus more as needed

¼ cup *extra virgin olive oil*, plus more as needed

Special Equipment: Food processor or blender

1. Cut each chile in half and remove the seeds. If your skin is sensitive, wear protective gloves. For a slightly milder schug, trim out and discard the ribs and seeds. Coarsely chop the chiles.

2. Transfer to the bowl of a food processor or the jar of a blender. Add the garlic, cumin, coriander, cardamom, salt, cilantro, and parsley. Pulse a few times, until coarsely chopped. Pulsing constantly, gradually add the lemon juice. Continue to pulse and gradually add the oil, then process until the mixture is well blended. Season with additional salt, lemon juice, or oil as needed. Transfer to a tightly covered container and refrigerate to meld the flavors, at least 2 hours. The schug can be refrigerated for up to 1 week. For longer storage, pour enough additional oil over the surface to a depth of about ¼ inch [6mm]. The flavor will continue to develop and mellow over time.

VARIATION

RED SCHUG: Substitute fresh red chilies, such as Fresno or red jalapeño, for the green chilies. Decrease the chopped cilantro to ½ cup. Substitute red wine vinegar for the lemon juice. Makes about 2 cups.

GIRLS' NIGHT

You don't need a reason to plan a girls' night out. It could be a special occasion like an engagement, a baby announcement, celebrating a new job (or just to wear your new Moda dress). There have even been times when I've gotten my RHONY girls together to watch an episode and make fun of ourselves. But usually, it's just a chance to gather friends that I haven't seen in a while and for us all to catch up. And I love spending time with my girls more than anything.

FIRST, establish if this is going to be a night in or the beginning of an evening out so your guests know how to dress, and you know what to serve. It can be a jeans-and-sweatshirt night of snacky food in front of the TV, or it can be the first act of a night on the town, enjoying the main meal at a restaurant. My friends tend to dress up because we never know where the evening will lead. This lack of predictability sparks the entire party. All we need is one person to say, *"Let's just go grab a drink at Chez Margeaux,"* and we're downstairs grabbing taxis . . .

FOR A CASUAL NIGHT IN, the idea is to hang back, but it might take a bit more responsibility on the part of the host to pull it together. I put out a big spread of our favorite foods and drinks, maybe a pitcher of Mezcalitas (see page 189) and/or a Dirty Martini (see page 193) setup. I consider this approach a nighttime version of my "everlasting brunch." I keep the bowls filled and the drinks chilled, and everyone is happy. You can also take a potluck approach to relieve a little of the pressure off yourself.

Oftentimes I'll set up board games like Scrabble or Monopoly, so we have activities on hand while we're drinking (and gossiping). Additionally, I'll set up scattered groupings of conversation nooks with their own snacks so small groups can gather easily.

DON'T MAKE AN EXCUSE for getting together with the girls. Just do it! Girls' night is like my version of therapy!

3

CASUAL

Family

MEALS

FUN, CASUAL, *impromptu* GATHERINGS

have my heart. While I love the planning that goes into an "event" dinner, I'm even happier to go with the flow for a simple weeknight meal. My laidback approach to weeknight cooking really came in handy when my brother David moved in with me after he graduated college. That guy ate everything in the house! I would reach for an ingredient and discover that it had disappeared (into his mouth), so I often had to make do with what was left in the fridge and pantry. It brought home the notion that when the meal is made with love, it doesn't have to be fancy. The sight of a clean plate makes me happier than almost anything else I can think of.

My approach to everyday cooking goes back to my dad's weekly Shabbat dinners. The door to our apartment would be unlocked so anyone who wanted a hot meal and company could come on in. So many nights the siblings would look at each other and be like, "Who's that?" Dad would just have invited some neighbor he met in the lobby that day to join us. He wasn't a great cook, but he was an honest one. His specialty was what he called sofrito, but I now lovingly call it Divorced Dad's Chicken (see page 132), a kind of soupy chicken stew. Filling, hearty, and absolutely delicious, it brightened the mood of anyone who ate it. And the secret ingredient was the care and love he put into this simple recipe.

Sometimes the kids will come home after school with friends, and rather than send their buddies back to their families at dinner time, I'll call and invite the rest of their family over for a meal. Or we'll leave a Saturday afternoon birthday party and invite some friends back over to our place, and naturally a couple hours later everyone's hungry. It's a great way to make a dull evening into an instant party—if the homework gets done, I'm good with that. Don't sweat it—the meal does not have to be perfect. The idea is to spend time with your kids and their friends (and family), break bread together, and get to know everyone a little better. I swear that I find out more about what happens at school from my kid's friends than from my kids themselves.

From-Scratch
MAC AND CHEESE
with Broccoli

There are few more sure-fire, crowd-pleasing recipes than mac and cheese. There are tons of ways to make it, but I like this extra-creamy version "beefed up" with chunks of broccoli for extra vitamins. This recipe was literally how I got my kids to eat a cruciferous vegetable for years without knowing it. This isn't the baked kind with a crunchy topping, but I would totally be down to try it that way too.

PREP: **10 minutes** COOK: **About 20 minutes**

1 pound (454g) *cavatappi (corkscrew) pasta*

3 *broccoli crowns*, florets only (save the stems for another use)

4 tablespoons *unsalted butter*

4 tablespoons *all-purpose flour*

2 cups *whole milk*, warmed

1 cup *heavy cream*, warmed

3 cups freshly grated *sharp Cheddar*

½ cup freshly grated *Parmesan*, plus more for garnish

Kosher salt and freshly ground *black pepper*, to taste

Chopped *flat-leaf parsley*, for garnish

1. Bring a large pot of salted water to a boil over high heat. Add the cavatappi and cook according to the package instructions. About 2 minutes before the end of cooking, gradually stir the broccoli florets into the pot (so the water keeps boiling), and cook until pasta and broccoli are al dente. Reserve ½ cup of the pasta cooking water, then drain the pasta and broccoli.

2. Meanwhile, in a large skillet, heat the butter over medium heat until foaming. Whisk in the flour and cook until it is lightly toasted, 1 to 2 minutes. Gradually whisk in the warm milk and cream and bring to a simmer, whisking often. Reduce the heat to low, add the Cheddar and Parmesan, and whisk until melted and smooth. Season with salt and pepper. Add the pasta and broccoli and stir well.

3. Gradually stir in the reserved pasta cooking water until the sauce reaches your desired consistency. It should be nice and creamy.

4. Spoon into pasta bowls, sprinkle with the parsley, and an extra sprinkle of Parmesan, and serve hot.

LEMON PASTA
with Summer Squash and Cheese

There comes a time every summer when yellow and green summer squash and zesty, fragrant basil is everywhere. That's the best time to make this vegetarian pasta, but it can bring the taste of summer any time of year, too. I also use some of the pine nuts I've stored in the freezer or fridge to give a little crunch. It's one of the easiest and tastiest pasta dishes I know.

PREP: **10 minutes**   *COOK:* **About 25 minutes**

1 pound (450g) *pasta* (linguine, fettuccine, or spaghetti work well)

2 tablespoons *extra virgin olive oil*

2 tablespoons *unsalted butter*

3 small *yellow squash*, thinly sliced

3 small *zucchini*, thinly sliced

4 *garlic cloves*, minced

½ teaspoon *crushed red pepper* flakes

Zest and juice of 1 large *lemon*

1 cup freshly grated *Parmesan*

½ cup *pine nuts*, toasted

Kosher salt and freshly ground *black pepper*, to taste

½ cup crumbled *feta* or ricotta salata

Fresh basil leaves, torn, for garnish

1. Bring a large pot of salted water to a boil over high heat. Add the pasta and cook according to package directions until al dente. Reserve ½ cup of pasta cooking water, then drain the pasta and set aside.

2. In a large skillet, heat the oil and butter over medium-high heat. Add the sliced yellow squash and zucchini, sautéing until tender and lightly golden, 5 to 6 minutes. Add the garlic and crushed red pepper and cook until fragrant, 1 to 2 minutes. Add the lemon zest, lemon juice, and the pasta to the skillet, and toss well. If the pasta looks dry, add a splash of the reserved pasta cooking water until it reaches your desired consistency.

3. Sprinkle the Parmesan and pine nuts over the pasta and toss to coat. Season with salt and pepper. Sprinkle the feta or ricotta salata and the basil on top and serve.

LINGUINE
with Fresh Clams

The Hamptons are "clam country." You can dig them up yourself (with the right permit, mind you) or buy them from any number of enterprising clamdiggers. My spot is the Seafood Shop in Wainscott. I have to force myself not to make this every night when we're out there in the summer because of the amount of butter and bread I use. While a lot of cooks cheat with canned clams, it's SO much better with clams in the shell so you get lots of that briny juice. Be sure to scrub the clams like crazy to get any hidden sand off the shells. This is probably the most important step.

<u>PREP:</u> **35 to 45 minutes (including soaking time)**
<u>COOK:</u> **About 30 minutes**

4 pounds (1.8kg) *fresh littleneck clams*

Kosher salt

1 pound (454g) *linguine*

12 tablespoons *unsalted butter*, to taste (sometimes I get even more generous with the butter!)

6 *cloves garlic*, finely chopped

½ teaspoon *crushed red pepper*

Zest and juice of 1 *lemon*, plus more as needed, and 1 lemon, cut into wedges, for serving

2 cups *dry white wine*, such as Sauvignon Blanc, to taste

Freshly ground *black pepper*

¼ cup chopped *parsley* leaves and tender stems

1. Soak the clams in a large bowl of salty ice water to cover for 20 to 30 minutes. This helps them expel any sand or grit. Gently lift the clams out of the water and transfer them to a colander set in the sink. Don't pour the clams into the colander because the sand that has settled at the bottom of the bowl will end up back on the clams.

2. Rinse each clam under cold running water, and scrub, scrub, scrub the shells with a stiff brush to remove any remaining debris (I mean, *really* scrub them). Discard any clams with cracked shells or those that remain open after a light tap. Rinse *well*. Set aside.

3. Bring a large pot of salted water to a boil over high heat. Add the linguine and cook according to package directions until al dente. Reserve ½ cup of the pasta cooking water. Drain the pasta and set it aside.

4. Meanwhile, in a Dutch oven or large, deep skillet with a tight-fitting lid, melt the butter over medium heat. Add the garlic and red pepper flakes, cooking until the garlic is golden and fragrant, 1 to 2 minutes. Add the juice of ½ lemon and the wine. Increase the heat to medium-high and bring to a simmer.

5. Add the clams. Tightly cover the skillet with its lid. Bring to a boil and cook until all the clams have opened, 5 to 7 minutes. Use a slotted spoon or spider to transfer the clams to a large bowl; discard any clams that remain closed.

6. Add the reserved lemon juice, grated zest, and parsley to the clam cooking liquid. Pour a little of it over the clams.

7. Put the drained pasta into a large bowl, pour the remaining sauce over it, and toss to coat. Taste and add more lemon juice if needed. Season with salt and black pepper.

8. Place the two bowls of clams and pasta on the table. Serve with the lemon wedges.

Grandma-Style PAN PIZZA

Making pizza can be a lot of fun, but rolling out the dough and using a pizza stone isn't for everyone. This version uses a sheet pan and a conventional oven. This recipe calls for my Kubaneh dough, which adds a flakiness and fluffiness to the pizza that's both unusual and delicious. Stretching the dough right into a pan is the unfussy way that many Italian grandmas make their pizza at home. I'm recommending a vegetarian topping, but you can use whatever you want. Two tips, though: All vegetables (especially squashes and mushrooms) should be cooked before using because raw veggies will give off their juices and make the dough soggy. Also, don't overload the toppings.

PREP: **30 to 40 minutes (including dough resting times)**
COOK: **About 30 minutes**

1× batch **Kubaneh dough** (see page 59), through the first rise

Extra-virgin olive oil, for coating

FOR THE TOPPING

Extra virgin olive oil, for drizzling

2 cups **marinara sauce**, plain tomato sauce, or drained, canned chopped roasted tomatoes

2 **cloves garlic**, if using plain tomato sauce or canned tomatoes

8 to 10 slices **Fried Eggplant** (see page 95, optional)

1 or 2 **broccoli crowns**, florets only, blanched (see Note) and coarsely chopped (optional)

A large handful of pitted **Kalamata olives**, coarsely chopped (optional)

½ cup crumbled **feta** (optional)

2 cups **shredded mozzarella**

¼ cup freshly grated **Parmesan**

Fresh basil leaves

Crushed hot red pepper (optional)

Special Equipment: 10×13-inch (25×2.5cm) half-sheet pan or similar large, rimmed baking sheet.

1. Preheat the oven to 500°F (260°C). Lightly grease a half-sheet pan with some oil.

2. Place the dough on the baking sheet and gently stretch and pull it into a large rectangular shape that almost fills the pan. Cover with a clean kitchen towel and let it rest for 10 minutes.

3. Stretch it out again toward the edges of the pan, this time filling to the corners. If it springs back, cover with the towel and let it rest for 10 minutes, then try again.

4. Drizzle the dough with olive oil. If using tomato sauce or canned tomatoes, stir in the garlic. Spread the tomato sauce over the pizza, leaving a 1-inch (2.5cm) border. Scatter over the mozzarella and Parmesan evenly. If using toppings, arrange the eggplant, broccoli, olives, and feta on top of the cheese.

5. Bake the pizza until the cheese is melted and the crust is nicely browned, about 30 minutes. Drizzle with more olive oil. Tear the basil leaves over the pizza and sprinkle with hot red pepper. Cut into big rectangles and serve immediately.

NOTE *To blanch the broccoli, bring a medium saucepan of salted water to a boil over high heat. Add the broccoli florets and cook just until crisp-tender and bright green, 2 to 3 minutes. Drain, rinse under cold water to stop the cooking, and drain again. Pat dry with a clean kitchen towel.*

Cheese
SAMBUSAK

Sambusak comes from the Persian word sanbosag, meaning "beautiful triangle," which is exactly what these little pastries are. I grew up having these around the house at all times, no exaggeration. My grandmother stayed making sambusak! Her big hands were always kneading dough and she never skimped on the cheese. I make them with my kids as a family project, and it makes me so happy to see the comfort that cooking together at home brings. You can serve them as an appetizer or just always have them around for a grab-and-go snack like we do. I literally can never keep up with how many I need to have around so I just make a huge batch and hope it lasts more than 3 days.

PREP: 1 hour and 15 minutes (including dough resting time)   *COOK:* 40 to 45 minutes

3 cups **all-purpose flour**, plus more for rolling the dough

1 teaspoon **kosher salt**

½ cup **unsalted butter**, melted and cooled

½ cup **vegetable oil**

½ cup hot water

4 ounces (115g) **feta cheese**, broken into chunks

4 ounces (115g) **low-moisture mozzarella**, torn into rough pieces

1 cup freshly grated **Parmesan**

3 **large eggs**, divided

2 tablespoons **sesame seeds**, for topping (optional)

Special Equipment: Food processor

1. In a large bowl, whisk together the flour and salt. Make a well in the middle and pour the butter, oil, and ½ cup hot water into the well. Stir the liquid gently, bringing in a little of the flour with each rotation. When the mixture becomes too stiff to stir, use your hands to knead it into a smooth dough. Cover the bowl with a damp kitchen towel and let the dough rest for 30 minutes.

2. Add the feta, mozzarella, Parmesan, and 2 of the eggs to the bowl of a food processor. Run the processor until the cheese filling is very well blended.

3. Preheat the oven to 350°F (180°C). Line two baking sheets with parchment paper.

4. Lightly flour a work surface. Have both the dough and the cheese filling ready. Pull off a piece of dough that is about 1½ inches (4cm) around and press it into a small disk. Use a rolling pin to roll it out to a roughly 5-inch (12cm) circle; the dough will be very thin.

5. Place 2 teaspoons of cheese filling in the center of the round. Gently fold the dough in half, enclosing the cheese and press the edges of the dough together. Use a sharp knife to trim off the rough ends (reserve the trimmed scraps), making sure to leave a ¼-inch to ½ -inch [6 mm to 12mm] edge. Press the edge with the tines of a fork to seal and decorate it.

6. Place the sambusak on a prepared baking sheet. Repeat to use all of the dough, rerolling the scraps, and the cheese filling.

7. Arrange the sambusak about ½ inch (12mm) apart on the baking sheets. Whisk the remaining egg with 1 tablespoon of water for an egg wash. Brush the tops and sprinkle with the sesame seeds, if desired.

8. Bake until light golden brown, 40 to 45 minutes. Let cool on the pan and serve warm. Sambusak are best eaten the day they are made. Leftovers can be stored in a tightly closed container at room temperature for up to 2 days.

Eden Grinshpan's FAMILY-STYLE BOUREKA BRAID

Bourekas are usually made individually but my friend and talented chef/television host, Eden Grinshpan, taught me how to make a single large pastry braid that is suitable for large gatherings. When I say my mouth was watering when I tried this, I'm being literal. You can watch the Instagram reel we made together if you don't believe me. She makes hers with a cheese filling like the one for the Sambusak on page 122, and it's perfection.

<u>PREP:</u> **30 minutes (including chilling time)**
<u>COOK:</u> **35 to 45 minutes**

2× 7-ounce (200g) packages *sheep's milk feta*

½ cup *whole milk ricotta*, drained in a wire sieve for at least 10 minutes

1 cup *shredded low-moisture mozzarella*

2 large *eggs*, divided

Freshly ground *black pepper*

All-purpose flour, for rolling out the dough

1× 14-ounce (396g) package *frozen puff pastry*, thawed

1 tablespoon *sesame seeds*, for garnish

FOR SERVING

Shabbat Eggs (see page 44), sliced

Sliced *radishes* and *sliced fennel*, drizzled with *extra virgin olive oil* and sprinkled with *flaky salt*

Shaved Tomatoes (see page 52) mixed with a few tablespoons of *Schug* (see page 104)

1. To make the filling, crumble the feta into a large bowl. Add the drained ricotta and mozzarella. Lightly whisk 1 of the eggs and add it to the bowl along with a few grinds of pepper. Stir until evenly blended.

2. Line a baking sheet with parchment paper. Lightly dust a work surface with flour. Roll out the puff pastry to a rectangle about 10×16 inches (25×40.5cm). Transfer it to the prepared baking sheet.

3. Spread the filling lengthwise down the center of the dough, leaving a border of 1 inch (2.5cm) at the top and bottom and a border of 3 inches (7.5cm) on the two long sides.

4. Using a sharp knife or pizza cutter, cut 8 slanting lines down one long side, cutting from the pastry edge to about ¾ inch from the filling to make strips about 1½ inches (4cm) wide. Repeat on the other side, making strips directly opposite the first cuts. Fold the top and bottom ends over the filling; trim the excess dough on either side of each flap that is not enclosing the filling. Fold the strips across the center, alternating strips from each side and crisscrossing them over the filling.

5. Meanwhile, preheat the oven to 375°F (190°C). Whisk the remaining egg with 1 tablespoon of water. Brush the top of the pastry with some of the egg wash. Sprinkle the sesame seeds on top. Bake until golden brown, 35 to 45 minutes.

6. Transfer to a large platter and cool slightly. Slide onto a large platter. Surround with the radishes and fennel, drizzle with the oil, and sprinkle with the flaky salt. Add the sliced eggs. Serve warm with tomato spread passed on the side. The braid is best eaten the day it is made. Leftovers can be refrigerated in an airtight container for up to 1 day. Bring to room temperature before eating.

CHICKEN AND BROCCOLI SAUTÉ
with Rice and Toppings

This is a super-easy chicken and broccoli dish for the kiddos! It's quick, balanced, and nutritious. They love it. And honestly everyone does. Serve with rice, if desired, and you're set for dinner.

PREP: **10 minutes**   *COOK:* **15 minutes**

2 tablespoons *vegetable oil*, plus more as needed

2 pounds (910g) *boneless skinless kosher chicken breast*, sliced into 2× ½-inch (5×1.2cm) strips

1½ teaspoons *onion powder*

1 teaspoon *garlic powder*

1 teaspoon *dry adobo seasoning*

½ teaspoon *sweet paprika*

1 pound (54g) *broccoli crowns*, florets only (stems reserved for another use)

¼ cup *soy sauce*, plus more for serving

1 tablespoon *toasted sesame oil*

Kosher salt and freshly ground *black pepper*

Cooked rice, for serving

FOR THE TOPPINGS

Baby spinach

Toasted sesame seeds

Sliced *scallions*, white and green parts

Coarsely chopped *roasted peanuts* or cashews

1. In a large mixing bowl, toss the sliced chicken breast with onion powder, garlic powder, adobo seasoning, and sweet paprika until well coated.

2. Heat 2 tablespoons vegetable oil in a large skillet or wok over medium-high heat. Add the chicken to the skillet in a single layer, and cook, stirring occasionally, until barely cooked through and golden brown, 6 to 8 minutes. Transfer to a bowl.

3. In the same pan, add a bit more oil if needed, and add the broccoli florets. Cook, stirring occasionally, until the broccoli is bright green and just tender-crisp, 3 to 4 minutes.

4. Return the chicken to the pan, and add soy sauce and toasted sesame oil, stirring well to coat everything evenly. Cook, stirring occasionally, to meld the flavors, about 2 minutes.

5. To serve, spoon the rice into soup bowls and top with the chicken and broccoli. Serve with bowls of the baby spinach, toasted sesame seeds, sliced scallions, and chopped nuts for everyone to customize their bowls as they like.

Kosher POULTRY *and* HOME DRY-BRINING

Kosher poultry has a reputation for tasting better. This is because the birds are salted during processing, which seasons them. But if you can't source kosher poultry as easily as I can, the solution is to salt a non-kosher bird at home. It's easy to do.

Start by rinsing the chicken or turkey well under cold running water, leaving the clinging water on the surface. For every pound of poultry, combine 2 tablespoons of kosher salt, preferably Diamond Crystal, and 1 teaspoon of granulated sugar. (Turkey T'bit, another family recipe using a whole bird, has different proportions; see the recipe on page 154.) Sprinkle this all over the poultry, and inside of a whole bird. Let stand on a wire rack over a baking sheet at room temperature (you can refrigerate it) for 1 hour. Rinse again. Pat dry with paper towels. It's not the same as koshering but approximates the flavor.

YEMENITE SOUP

This soup is our Yemenite penicillin, because its restorative powers will cure whatever ails you. Literally. We make this a few times a month in the winter and when Levi comes home from school, walks in the door, gets a whiff of the spices simmering and yells, "OH BET, Yemenite Soup!" I know I did good. While we always serve this with a side of basmati rice, it doesn't stop my kids from adding a big handful of Osem croutons to their bowl. It is also perfect with Kubaneh (which is how it's traditionally served in Israel) because what's soup without bread (see page 59)?

PREP: **15 minutes**   COOK: **7 hours and 15 minutes**

4 pounds (1.8kg) **boneless beef chuck**, cut into 1½-in (4cm) cubes or bone-in skinless kosher chicken thighs and legs

1½ tablespoons **kosher salt**

1 teaspoon freshly ground **black pepper**

4 tablespoons **vegetable oil**, as needed

2 large **russet potatoes**, peeled and left whole

2 large **tomatoes**, halved

2 whole **jalapeños** or other fresh green chiles (optional)

1 large **yellow onion**, peeled and left whole

4 **cloves garlic**, peeled and left whole

1 bunch **fresh cilantro**, tied with kitchen twine

2 tablespoons **Hawaij** (see page 98)

2 tablespoons **beef or chicken bouillon paste**

FOR SERVING

Basil leaves

Soup croutons, such as Osem, or small soup crackers

Cooked basmati rice

Kubaneh (see page 59) or Lachuch (see page 83)

1. Place the beef cubes or chicken pieces on a baking sheet and season with the salt and pepper.

2. If using beef, in a large pot or Dutch oven, heat 2 tablespoons of oil over medium-high heat until shimmering. In batches, without crowding, add the beef and cook, turning occasionally, until browned, about 8 minutes, transferring the beef to a bowl, and adding more oil as needed.

3. Pour out the fat and wipe the pot clean. Return the beef to the pot or, if using chicken, add it to the pot. Add the potatoes, tomatoes, jalapenos (if using), onion, garlic, and cilantro. Sprinkle in the Hawaij. Pour in enough water to cover all the ingredients and stir in the bouillon paste.

4. Bring the pot to a gentle boil over medium heat. Reduce the heat to very low. Cover tightly and let the soup simmer until the beef or chicken and potatoes are falling-apart tender, about 7 hours. Season with additional salt and pepper.

5. Using the side of a serving spoon, break the vegetables into serving portions. Ladle the soup into soup bowls. Tear the basil into small pieces and let fall into the soup. Serve hot, with the croutons, rice, and kubaneh or lachuch on the side.

MAHASHA *(Stuffed Bell Peppers)*

This is an easy dish that presents itself really nicely. It's a staple in Iraqi meals and the spices that are mixed into the meat blend so nicely with the cooked peppers (or the onions). In my personal opinion, the onions taste better but the peppers are more traditional and look nicer so it's really up to you to choose. You can also make a combo of both!

PREP: **20 minutes**   *COOK:* **30 to 40 minutes**

FOR THE STUFFED PEPPERS

6 medium *green or red bell peppers*

1 pound (450g) *ground beef*

2 cups *cooked basmati rice* (from about ⅔ cup uncooked rice)

½ *yellow onion*, finely chopped

1× 14.5-ounce (411g) *can of diced tomatoes* or 2 cups chopped ripe, fresh tomatoes

¼ cup *pine nuts*, lightly toasted

1 teaspoon *sweet paprika*

½ teaspoon *ground cumin*

½ teaspoon *ground cinnamon*

1 teaspoon *kosher salt*

½ teaspoon freshly ground *black pepper*

Chopped *flat-leaf parsley*, for garnish

FOR THE TOMATO SAUCE

2 tablespoons *extra virgin olive oil*

2 *cloves garlic*, minced

2× 15-ounce (425g) cans of *tomato sauce*

1 teaspoon *beef or chicken bouillon paste*

1½ teaspoons *dried oregano*

Kosher salt and freshly ground *black pepper*

1. To prepare the peppers, cut off the top ½ inch (12mm) of each pepper and a very thin slice from the bottoms so that they stand. Discard the stems, seeds, and ribs. Finely chop the top "caps" and place in a large bowl. Rinse the peppers and set aside.

2. To the chopped pepper, add the beef, rice, onion, tomatoes, pine nuts, paprika, cumin, cinnamon, salt, and pepper. Stir to combine. Spoon the beef mixture into each pepper, packing it slightly. Set aside on a platter.

3. To make the sauce, in a large Dutch oven or deep skillet with a lid, heat the olive oil and garlic over medium heat until the garlic is tender, about 2 minutes. Stir in 1 cup water, the tomato sauce, bouillon paste, and oregano. Season with salt and pepper. Bring the sauce to a simmer over medium heat. Carefully place the peppers in the simmering tomato sauce, being sure they are partially submerged.

4. Cover and reduce the heat to low. Simmer until the peppers are tender, 30 to 40 minutes. Using a slotted spoon, transfer each pepper to a soup bowl. Spoon the tomato sauce over each, sprinkle with parsley, and serve.

VARIATION

STUFFED ONIONS: Substitute 6 large yellow or sweet onions, peeled, for the bell peppers. Trim the root ends slightly (but do not cut off the root!) so the onions do not roll. Bring a large pot of salted water to a boil. Add the onions and cook until tender enough to separate the layers but still firm, 10 to 12 minutes. Drain and cool until easy to handle. Working with one onion at a time, carefully separate the onion layers, removing and setting aside the centers, leaving 2 or 3 of the outer layers attached at the bottom to form a "cup." Chop the onion trimmings to substitute for the half yellow onion in the filling. Proceed as directed.

Divorced Dad's
CHICKEN IN A POT

When my dad became a single father to my younger siblings, he didn't know how to cook anything. He taught himself how to make this chicken dish, and we loved it so much that we've added it to our family's Shabbat menu rotation ever since. It's one of the easiest recipes you'll ever encounter, if you allow for four hours of cooking time. Sofrito is a finely chopped vegetable cooking base in Latin cuisine, and I have no idea how Dad got this name for his chicken in a pot, but that's what he called it.

PREP: **10 minutes**   COOK: **4 hours and 10 minutes**

4 pounds (1.8kg) **bone-in kosher chicken thighs**, **legs**, **and breasts**

Kosher salt and freshly ground **black pepper**

2 medium **yellow onion**s, cut into thin wedges

1 **head garlic**, cloves separated and peeled

1 pound (454g) **baby potatoes**, scrubbed

4 large **carrots**, peeled and cut into large chunks

1½ tablespoons **chicken bouillon paste**

1 teaspoon **sweet paprika**

½ teaspoon **cayenne pepper** (optional)

8 sprigs **flat-leaf parsley**, tied in a bunch with kitchen twine

1 **lemon**, thinly sliced

Cooked basmati rice, for serving

1. Preheat the oven to 325°F (165°C). Season the chicken pieces with a few pinches of salt and pepper and arrange them in a single layer in a large baking pan.

2. Add the onion, garlic, potatoes, and carrots to the pan, tucking the vegetables under and around and scattering them on top of the chicken.

3. Dissolve the bouillon paste in 3 cups of hot water and whisk in the paprika, cayenne, if desired, and 1 teaspoon each salt and pepper. Pour it into the pan. Tuck the parsley bundle and the lemon slices around the chicken.

4. Lay a piece of parchment paper on top of the ingredients, then cover the pan tightly with aluminum foil.

5. Bake for 4 hours or until the chicken is falling-apart tender. Remove the foil and the parchment and set under a high broiler for 10 minutes to brown the top.

6. Spoon the rice into bowls and add servings of the chicken, vegetables, and cooking liquid.

Spatchcocked
ROASTED CHICKEN
with Israeli Spices

Roast chicken is one of the cornerstones of good home cooking. There is nothing like bringing a juicy bird with golden brown skin to the table. If the chicken is spatchcocked (basically, butterflied), the skin is exposed to more of the oven heat, and you get more of that irresistibly crisp exterior. I cook the bird on a bed of sliced bread, which soaks up the spicy juices and becomes unbelievably delicious, a tip I learned from my best friend Calder Quinn's mom, Lucinda Scala Quinn. She is a big inspiration for me, as I grew up hanging out after school at their Riverside apartment overlooking the Hudson, nibbling on this dish very often. Give this a try when the craving for roast chicken hits. This recipe is perfect for using one of your homemade spice blends.

PREP: **10 minutes**   *COOK:* **About 1 hour**
TOTAL: **1 hour and 10 minutes**

1 **whole kosher chicken**, 3 to 4 pounds (1.4 to 1.8kg), spatchcocked (see Note)

4 tablespoons **unsalted butter**, softened

2 tablespoons **extra-virgin olive oil**

1½ tablespoons **Baharat** or Hawaij (see page 98)

1 teaspoon **kosher salt**

4 slices hearty **sourdough or country bread**, preferably day-old or stale, sliced at least ½-inch (12mm) thick

1 **lemon**, sliced

6 **cloves garlic**, peeled and lightly smashed under a knife

12 sprigs **fresh thyme** or 6 sprigs fresh rosemary, or a combination

Special Equipment: Instant-read thermometer

1. Preheat the oven to 425°F (220°C). Pat the chicken completely dry with paper towels.

2. In a small bowl, mix the butter, oil, baharat or hawaij, and salt to form a paste.

3. Rub the spice mixture generously over both sides of the chicken, ensuring an even coating, especially under the skin for maximum flavor.

4. Place the bread slices in a single layer in a large cast-iron skillet. Scatter the lemon, garlic, and fresh thyme or rosemary sprigs over and around the bread.

5. Place the chicken, skin-side up, on top of the bread. Roast until an instant-read thermometer inserted in the thickest part of the thigh reads 165°F (74°C), 50 to 55 minutes. For a crisper skin, broil the chicken for 2 to 3 minutes.

6. Let rest for about 10 minutes. Cut into serving pieces in the skillet and serve with the pan juices, bread, and garlic.

NOTE   *Spatchcocked chickens are sold in some well-stocked grocery stores. To spatchcock a whole bird at home, place the chicken breast-side down on a cutting board. Using kitchen shears, cut along both sides of the backbone, from the tailbone up, and remove the backbone. (Save the backbone for another use, such as making broth.) Flip the chicken over and press down firmly on the breastbone with both hands, cracking the breastbone and flattening the chicken. Tuck the wing tips under the breasts to prevent burning.*

PICADILLO

Abe's mother, Reggie (Regla), often makes picadillo for Shabbat dinner, and it makes our main course rotation on a regular basis. This dish is comfort food and delicious, and your guests will definitely ask you for the recipe. My mother-in-law's picadillo is a "frills-free" version. But other cooks like to add a handful each of raisins and sliced pimiento-stuffed green olives for a sweet-and-salty effect, and garnish with sliced hard-boiled eggs. You know what I say—make it your way! But from all the versions I've tasted I have to be honest, this one's the best.

PREP: **20 minutes** _COOK:_ **40 to 50 minutes**

2 tablespoons _extra-virgin olive oil_

2 pounds (910g) _ground beef_

2 teaspoons _kosher salt_, plus more as needed

¾ teaspoon freshly ground _black pepper_

3 cups homemade or store-bought _marinara_ or other tomato sauce, or as needed

1 _green bell pepper_, seeded and coarsely chopped

4 _scallions_, coarsely chopped

1 head of _garlic cloves_, coarsely chopped

1½ lightly packed cups _fresh cilantro leaves_ and tender stems (about 1 bunch)

Cooked basmati rice, for serving

Platanos (see page 87), for serving

Tostones (see page 88), for serving

1. Heat the olive oil in a large skillet over medium heat. Add the ground beef and the salt and pepper. Cook, stirring occasionally, breaking up the meat with the side of a spoon, until most of the pink is gone, about 8 minutes.

2. Meanwhile, in a bowl of a food processor, pulse the green pepper, scallions, garlic, cilantro, and a pinch of salt until coarsely chopped. Add the marinara and the meat to the vegetables and pulse a few times to combine. (Or, using a large, sharp knife, finely chop the vegetables on a chopping board. Transfer to a large mixing bowl, add the beef mixture and marinara, and stir well.)

3. Return the mixture to the skillet and bring to a simmer over medium-low heat. Cook, stirring often, until the vegetables are very tender, 30 to 40 minutes. Season with salt and pepper.

4. Serve hot, spooned over rice with Platanos and Tostones.

TEAM EFFORT

There are times when cooking by myself is just what the doctor ordered: Chopping, stirring, and tasting with some great music in the background and a glass of red is a way for me to soothe my soul. And I know I'm not alone in this feeling.

But there's a lot of fun to be had when I cook with a group of friends and family. Just remember, you're going to be bumping into each other, so your attitude has to be chill. To make a last-minute meal happen, take an "all-hands-on-deck" approach. Make something where a few extra hands will make the prep go quickly. Use this opportunity to roll mountains of Meatballs (see page 161), fold a few dozen Sambusaks (see page 122), or roll a batch of Moroccan cigars (see page 80). My kids love being a part of rolling the overnight Jachnun rolls (page 55)—I'll make the filling and sauce while the rest of the crew does the folding and rolling.

　　All the food doesn't have to be eaten that night, and if you freeze some of it for another meal, you're ready for the next on-the-fly dinner you have. Put friends and family who are less comfortable cooking to work in setting the table, cleaning up, or keeping the tunes running on the playlist. I love both cooking alone and having people around to help.

4

GATHERINGS

I LOVE *the feeling of* DRESSING UP *for an* EVENT.

I've walked enough red carpets to know how great that feeling can be. And hosting a special event at home is honestly no different (and in many ways, it's even better.) Having a fancy dinner party means getting yourself glammed up in a great look that's both functional and stylish. I also like to match my theme, not overtly but as a nod to it—whether it's Thanksgiving in a romper and cozy sweater or my husband's 40th birthday party in a festive dress.

I apply the concept of "casual elegance," to all my large gatherings and special occasions. If you look at the recipes in this chapter, they are not especially fancy. There are reasons for this. No one (especially the host) likes a meal where the cook is stuck in the kitchen. (There's another reason, too. The host may be dressed up and not able to cook with the same sense of abandon as with a casual, everyday meal.) Keep the food simple and doable, and let your setting do the heavy lifting. A beautifully set table, laden with an array of carefully curated textures and colors, lit with soft candles, enhanced with a lovely floral arrangement—all of these will work together to elevate the food, even if it's one of your grandmother's recipes. Basically, I'm saying that there are more elements to a party that make it special aside from just the food . . . as important as that may be. This is a cookbook, yes, but also a guide to all aspects of giving a party. And I love a good party.

A satisfying feeling of abundance also goes a long way in setting the mood for a festive occasion. I don't serve individual portions on a plate—that's for restaurants and chefs in white jackets. Instead, I go for big platters heaping with food, bowls filled to the brim, large pots that give off an enticing aroma when you lift the lid. I appreciate a complex dish with three sauces when I am at a fine restaurant, but at home, there are other ways to please the senses than arranging bits of herbs with a pair of tweezers. Big, bold, and beautiful—that's how I host!

Throughout the book you'll find other ideas for how I like to organize my parties: setting up nooks for conversation, using lighting that complements your guests, rearranging your space for everyone's comfort. If you choose a menu that's appealing to the eye and palate but easy on the cook, you're halfway to a successful gathering. The other half is using your creativity and sense of artistry to set the scene to accomplish that casual elegance that is the real secret ingredient to being a perfect host (and having good mood lighting and music of course).

COUSCOUS *with Vegetables*

A big platter of steaming couscous topped with healthy, spiced vegetables—it doesn't get more photo-ready than that. When you have guests who are vegetarian or vegan, this is THE recipe to go for. While it's a warming dish for a cool autumn night, it's also good in the summer when you have lots of leftover veggies from the local farmstand. Keep the vegetables chopped chunky, and make sure not to overcook so they keep their shape. In keeping with the seasonal spirit, feel free to swap in whatever veggies happen to be in season where you are.

<u>PREP:</u> **20 minutes**   <u>COOK:</u> **About 45 minutes**

4 tablespoons *extra-virgin olive oil*, divided, plus more for serving

1 large *yellow onion*, chopped

4 *cloves garlic*, minced

1½ teaspoons *ground cumin*

1 teaspoon *smoked paprika*

½ teaspoon *ground coriander*

¼ teaspoon *ground turmeric*

2× 10.75 ounce (305g) cans of *crushed tomatoes*

2 tablespoons *vegetable bouillon paste*, divided

2 medium *zucchini*, cut into 2-inch (5cm) pieces

2 *yellow squashes*, cut into 2-inch (5cm) pieces

2 *bell peppers* (any color), cut into 2-inch (5cm) pieces

3 large *carrots*, cut into 1-inch (2.5cm) pieces

1 large *sweet potato*, peeled and cut into 2-inch (5cm) pieces (optional)

2 cups thick-sliced *cabbage* (sliced before measuring, see Note; optional)

2× 15.5 ounce (439g) can of *chickpeas*, rinsed and drained (about 3 cups)

4 *plum tomatoes*, cut into 2-inch (5cm) pieces

2 teaspoons *kosher salt*, plus more as needed

½ teaspoon freshly ground *black pepper*, plus more as needed

Finely grated zest and juice of 1 *lemon*

2 cups *couscous*

¼ cup chopped *flat-leaf parsley* leaves and tender stems

¼ cup chopped *fresh cilantro leaves* and tender stems

¼ cup *pine nuts* or slivered almonds, toasted (optional)

1. In a Dutch oven or other large pot, heat 3 tablespoons of the oil over medium-high heat. Add the onion and cook, stirring occasionally, until soft and translucent, about 7 minutes. Stir in the garlic, cumin, smoked paprika, coriander, and turmeric and cook until fragrant, about 1 minute. Stir in the crushed tomatoes, 1 tablespoon bouillon paste, and 2 cups of water. Bring to a boil, then reduce the heat and simmer for 5 minutes. The consistency should be soupy.

2. Add the zucchini, yellow squash, bell peppers, carrots, sweet potato (if using), and cabbage (if using). Cook, stirring occasionally, until the vegetables are cooked, 15 to 20 minutes.

3. Stir in the chickpeas and tomatoes and cook until heated through, about 5 minutes. Remove the Dutch oven from the heat and stir in the lemon zest and juice.

4. Meanwhile, for the couscous, bring 2 cups water to a boil in a large pot. Add the remaining 1 tablespoon of bouillon paste, the remaining 1 tablespoon of oil, ½ teaspoon salt, and the pepper. Stir in the couscous. Cover tightly, remove from the heat, and let stand until the couscous absorbs the liquid, about 5 minutes. Fluff with a fork and set aside, covered.

5. To serve, place the couscous and vegetables in separate platters or shallow serving bowls. Sprinkle the vegetables with parsley, cilantro, and pine nuts or almonds, if desired. Drizzle a bit of extra olive oil over the top. Serve warm or at room temperature.

NOTE *To prepare the cabbage, cut a head of cabbage lengthwise in half. Remove and discard the core from one of the cabbage halves and place it cut side down on the cutting board. Slice lengthwise into long strips that are 1-inch (2cm) wide.*

MOM'S RED RICE
with Almonds and Raisins

This is such a tasty side dish that just may steal the show from the main course. My mom makes this all the time. It's especially useful when you want to add an extra splash of color to the plate. We serve it warm for ease and as a complement to a hot dish, but you could also serve it hot.

PREP: **5 minutes**   COOK: **38 to 48 minutes**

2 cups *basmati rice*, rinsed and drained

1 cup *tomato sauce*

2 tablespoons *tomato paste*

1 tablespoon *chicken or other flavor bouillon paste*

2 teaspoons *kosher salt*, divided

½ teaspoon freshly ground *black pepper*, divided

½ cup *sliced almonds*

2 tablespoons *extra-virgin olive oil*

1 large *yellow onion*, chopped

½ cup *seedless raisins*

1. In a large saucepan, stir 3½ cups of water with the rice, tomato sauce, tomato paste, bouillon paste, 1 teaspoon salt, and ¼ teaspoon pepper to dissolve the bouillon and tomato pastes. Bring to a boil over high heat. Reduce the heat to low, cover tightly, and simmer until the rice is tender and the liquid is absorbed, 15 to 20 minutes. Remove from the heat and let stand, covered, for 5 minutes. Uncover, fluff with a fork, and let cool.

2. Meanwhile, put the almonds in a separate skillet over medium heat. Cook, stirring often, until toasted, about 3 minutes. Transfer to a plate. Add the oil to the skillet and heat it. Add the onion, the remaining salt, and remaining pepper and cook, stirring occasionally, until browned, about 15 minutes. Stir in the almonds. Remove from the heat and stir in the raisins. Let cool.

3. Once the rice has cooled, fold in the onion and almond mixture. Transfer to a serving bowl and serve at room temperature.

MOM'S BASMATI RICE
with Lima Beans and Dill

Another fabulous rice side dish from my mom. This one is her specialty. When hosting a big meal, it's nice to have vanity when it comes to rice side dishes. Especially when rice pairs so nicely with the larger dishes we serve. This one is particularly good with a meat dish.

PREP: **5 minutes**   COOK: **20 minutes**

2 cups *basmati rice*, rinsed and drained

1 tablespoon *extra virgin olive oil*

1 tablespoon *kosher salt*

1 pound (454g) *frozen lima beans*, rinsed under cold water to partially thaw

¾ cup finely chopped *fresh dill*, plus dill fronds for garnish

¼ teaspoon freshly ground *black pepper*

1. In a large saucepan, combine 3½ cups of water with the rice, oil, and salt. Bring to a boil over high heat. Reduce the heat to low, cover tightly, and simmer for 5 minutes.

2. Stir in the lima beans and the dill, cover again, and simmer until the rice is tender and the liquid is absorbed, 10 to 15 minutes. Remove from the heat and let stand, covered, for 5 minutes. Fluff with a fork. Transfer to a serving bowl, garnish with the dill fronds and pepper and serve warm.

BASMATI RICE
with Onion and Pine Nuts

Iraqis make so many different rice dishes. On any given holiday, my family will have 3 to 4 on the table. The nuts are an important component in this recipe—they aren't just a sprinkle for garnish. I like to serve this with a lamb or poultry main course, as the savory onion flavor and buttery nuts will complement the protein perfectly!

PREP: **10 minutes**   COOK: **32 to 40 minutes**

2 cups *basmati rice*, rinsed and drained

2 tablespoons *extra-virgin olive oil*, plus ¾ cup for the onions

1 tablespoon *chicken or vegetable bouillon paste*, such as Better than Bouillon

2 large *white onions*, chopped very finely

2 cups *pine nuts*

1 teaspoon *kosher salt*, or to taste

1 teaspoon freshly ground *black pepper*

1 teaspoon *sweet paprika* (optional)

Pinch of *ground turmeric* (optional)

Pinch of *ground cayenne* (optional)

Chopped *flat-leaf parsley*, for garnish

Special Equipment: Mortar and pestle or food processor

1. In a large saucepan, combine 2½ cups of water with the rice, 2 tablespoons of the oil, and the bouillon paste. Bring to a boil over high heat. Reduce the heat to low, cover tightly, and simmer until the rice is tender and the liquid is absorbed, 15 to 20 minutes. Remove from the heat and let stand, covered, for 5 minutes. Fluff with a fork, cover again, and set aside to keep warm.

2. Meanwhile, heat the remaining ¾ cup oil in a large skillet over medium heat. Add the onions and cook, stirring occasionally, until soft and translucent, 12 to 15 minutes. In a mortar and pestle or food processor, coarsely crush the pine nuts. Stir the pine nuts, salt, and pepper into the onions along with the paprika, turmeric, and cayenne, if desired. Stir to combine and cook over medium-low heat until heated through.

3. Fold the onion and pine nut mixture into the warm rice. Taste and adjust the seasoning. Transfer to a serving bowl. Sprinkle with the parsley and serve hot.

The Best CHICKEN SCHNITZEL *You'll Ever Have*

This is another Shabbat dish that makes a regular appearance on many Friday nights, and it was pretty much the only reason my dad would come over. This is another one the kids love. Oftentimes I'll make a batch in thin strips so it's easier for the littles to handle. I warn you—they will disappear, no matter how many you make! I've found that my two-step process, with a brief chilling time between the frying and baking, helps the savory crumb coating cling to the chicken. Don't skimp on the oil in the skillet as a little slick of it will not set the crust.

PREP: **15 minutes**   COOK: **About 2 hours (including chilling time)**   TOTAL: **2 hours and 15 minutes**

2 pounds (900g) *boneless, skinless kosher chicken breasts*

3 large *eggs*

1 cup *dry breadcrumbs*

1 cup *panko breadcrumbs*

2 tablespoons *sesame seeds* (optional)

1 teaspoon *dry adobo seasoning*

1 teaspoon *kosher salt*

½ teaspoon freshly ground *black pepper*

½ teaspoon *ground cayenne* (optional)

Vegetable or *olive oil*, for frying, plus more as needed (I like to use avocado oil)

Chopped *flat-leaf parsley*, for garnish

1 *lemon*, cut into wedges, for serving

Special Equipment: Instant read thermometer

1. Place each chicken breast between two pieces of plastic wrap or parchment paper on a sturdy work surface. Gently pound each with a meat mallet or rolling pin until it's about ½-inch (12mm) thick.

2. In a large bowl, whisk the eggs until frothy. On a large plate, combine the breadcrumbs, panko, sesame seeds, if desired, adobo, salt, pepper, and cayenne, if desired. Stir the mixture to break up any large clumps and set the plate aside.

3. Place a large platter or baking sheet at your work area. Working with one chicken breast at a time, dip it first into the whisked eggs, ensuring it's fully coated. Let any excess egg drip off, then press the chicken into the breadcrumb mixture. Turn it over and press down again to coat both sides evenly. Lightly shake off any excess breadcrumbs, then set the breaded chicken on the platter or baking sheet. Repeat with the remaining breasts.

4. Pour enough oil in a large deep skillet to come about ½ inch (12mm) up the sides. Heat over medium-high heat until the oil is hot and shimmering but not smoking, or 325°F (165°C) on an instant-read thermometer.

5. Line another baking sheet with paper towels. In batches, without crowding, add the chicken cutlets to the skillet. Fry until crisp and golden brown on the underside, 2 to 3 minutes. Flip and brown the other side, 2 to 3 minutes more. Adjust the heat as needed to keep the oil temperature steady. Transfer to the paper towels to drain. Continue with the remaining cutlets, adding and heating more oil as needed between batches. Let cool to room temperature.

6. After cooling, discard the paper towels and refrigerate the cutlets on the baking sheet until chilled, about 1 hour.

7. Preheat the oven to 325°F (160°C). Spread the chilled cutlets in a single layer on a baking sheet. Transfer to the oven and bake until the chicken shows no sign of pink when pierced with the tip of a small sharp knife, 50 to 60 minutes.

8. Arrange the schnitzel on a serving platter, sprinkle with parsley, and serve with lemon wedges on the side.

Grandma's TURKEY T'BIT

My grandma used to make every Thanksgiving meal with this turkey, and it was by far the most exciting dish on the table. The traditional way to make this dish is the Shabbat Chicken version (see the variation). Granted, because of the long cooking time, the rice does come out a bit soft, but that's just how we like it. When I made it for a Friendsgiving feast, my friends called it Middle Eastern congee after the Chinese rice dish. It has that similar consistency, and I swear it warms the soul! Disclaimer: You won't be able to go back to regular Thanksgiving Turkey after this.

PREP: **15 minutes**   COOK: **14 to 16 hours**

1 *whole kosher turkey* (14 to 16 pounds, 6.4 to 7.3kg), thawed if frozen

3 tablespoons *plant-based butter* (we use plant-based butter to be mindful of our kosher guests, but you can totally use regular)

3 tablespoons *kosher salt*, plus more as needed

1 teaspoon freshly ground *black pepper*, plus more as needed

4 large *yellow onions*, trimmed and peeled, divided

4 cups *basmati rice*

3 tablespoons *ground cumin*, to taste

2 tablespoon *garlic powder*, to taste

½ cup *extra-virgin olive oil*, plus more for coating the pan and turkey

1× 6-ounce (170g) can *tomato paste*

¼ cup *chicken bouillon paste*

1 *head garlic*, minced

8 large *eggs* (optional, for Shabbat Eggs, see page 44)

Chopped *flat-leaf parsley*, for garnish

Special Equipment: 16-inch (40.5cm) roasting pan

NOTE   *If using a non-kosher fresh turkey, increase the salt to 3 tablespoons kosher salt.*

1. Preheat the oven to 220°F (100°C). Lightly grease a 16-inch (40.5cm) roasting pan with oil.

2. Spread the butter under the skin of the turkey. Season inside the cavity with about one-third of the salt and pepper. Place one of the onions in the turkey cavity (cut it into wedges, if necessary, to fit), and rub the turkey all over with oil, then arrange it breast side up, in a large roasting pan. Generously season it all over with the remaining salt and pepper.

3. In a large, fine-mesh sieve, rinse the rice under cold running water until the water runs clear. Transfer to a large bowl. In a medium bowl, pour 1 cup (240ml) boiling water over the cumin and garlic powder. Stir in the ½ cup (120ml) olive oil, with the tomato paste, bouillon paste, and garlic. Pour the mixture over the rice along with 2 cups (480ml) water and stir to combine.

4. Spoon some of the rice mixture into the turkey cavity and spread the remaining rice in the pan, packing it all around the turkey. Pour an additional 3 cups of water over the rice and add some more salt, if desired.

5. Nestle 8 large eggs, if using, in the rice. Cover the pan tightly with its lid or aluminum foil.

6. Roast overnight (14 to 16 hours). Uncover the pan and let it stand for 20 minutes.

7. Serve directly from the pot or transfer the turkey (the meat will fall right off the bone, so no need to carve!) and rice to a large serving dish. Garnish with chopped parsley. Serve.

VARIATIONS

CHICKEN T'BIT WITH SHABBAT EGGS: The turkey is a once-a-year affair, but chicken t'bit is a regular part of our weekly shabbat. Roasting a chicken this way is just like roasting the turkey, and we even keep the same amount of rice most of the time, since it's so popular. You can use a regular large roasting pan for this. Substitute 1 whole (4 pound [1.8kg]) kosher chicken. Season it, inside and out, with 1 tablespoon kosher salt and 1 teaspoon freshly ground black pepper and use just 1 large onion. Cue the Shabbat Eggs: Just before covering the pan with foil, nestle 8 large eggs in the rice. Roast for 8 hours. Remove the eggs from the pan and serve them with the rest of the shabbat spread. Carve the chicken and serve it and the rice as above.

155

Sissy's
MOROCCAN FISH

This is a very classy and simple fish entrée with a wonderful North African flavor. It's a fantastic main course for a party because the vegetables the salmon is cooked in can be made ahead of time (and the aroma will welcome your guests into the kitchen). After that, it's just a matter of reheating it and slipping the fillets into the broth for a fast final cooking. Thanks to my sister for this recipe. Feel free to sub in other types of fish.

PREP: **10 minutes**   COOK: **About 1 hour**
TOTAL: **1 hour and 10 minutes**

¼ cup *extra-virgin olive oil*

1 large *yellow onion*, chopped

6 *cloves garlic*, finely chopped

Kosher salt and freshly ground *black pepper*

2 tablespoons *tomato paste*

1 tablespoon *sweet paprika*

¼ teaspoon *hot paprika*, or to taste (optional)

½ teaspoon *ground cumin*

½ teaspoon *ground turmeric*

2 *carrots*, coarsely chopped

1 large *russet potato*, peeled and coarsely chopped, or 8 ounces (226g) baby potatoes, scrubbed

1 *red bell pepper*, seeded and sliced into long strips

1 cup chopped fresh or drained canned *tomatoes*

1 *jalapeño* or other fresh chile, seeded, ribs removed, coarsely chopped (optional)

1 *lemon*, finely sliced

1 cup chopped *cilantro leaves* and tender stems, plus more for garnish

4 *salmon fillets*, about 6 ounces (170g) each

Cooked basmati rice, for serving

1 *lemon*, cut into wedges, for serving

1. Heat the oil in a large, deep skillet or Dutch oven over medium heat. Add the onion and cook, stirring often, until softened, about 7 minutes. Stir in the garlic and a pinch of salt, and cook until the onion is golden, about 2 minutes more.

2. Stir in the tomato paste, sweet paprika, hot paprika, if desired, cumin, and turmeric, and cook until the spices are fragrant and the paste deepens in color, about 1 minute.

3. Add the carrots, potatoes, and bell pepper, stir well. Season lightly with salt and pepper, then add the tomato, jalapeño, if desired, and the sliced lemon along with ½ cup (120ml) water. Stir everything together until combined, then cover and let simmer over medium-low heat until the potatoes and carrots are just tender, about 30 minutes, adding a little more water, if necessary, to keep the mixture saucy.

4. Nestle the salmon fillets into the sauce and spoon a bit of sauce and vegetables on top. Sprinkle with the cilantro, cover tightly, and simmer until the salmon is rosy pink when flaked in the thickest part, 8 to 10 minutes.

5. For each serving, add rice to a wide soup bowl, add a fish fillet and a portion of the sauce and vegetables. Sprinkle with the cilantro, add a lemon wedge, and serve.

EGGPLANT *and* SHIITAKE PARMESAN

Eggplant Parmesan is a versatile main course that can be the star at a family meal or a big social gathering. I stole this particular version from my MIL, Reggie, who would make this when she'd have just one or two of her 5 kids over for dinner. I love a nice fresh baguette to scoop the sauce with—Mmmm... Reggie's version includes meaty shiitake mushrooms with the eggplant for added variety.

PREP: 50 minutes (including draining time)
COOK: 1 hour and 25 minutes

2 large *eggplants*, about 2 pounds (910g) total, cut into ¼-inch (6mm) rounds

1 tablespoon *kosher salt*, plus more as needed

Extra virgin olive oil, for frying and the sauce

1 medium *yellow onion*, finely chopped

3 *cloves garlic*, finely chopped

1½ pound (680g) *shiitake mushrooms*, stems discarded, caps sliced

1× 28-ounce (794g) can of *crushed tomatoes*

1 teaspoon *sugar*

½ teaspoon *dried basil*

½ teaspoon *dried oregano*

½ teaspoon *crushed red pepper*, or to taste (optional)

Freshly ground *black pepper*

2 cups *shredded low-moisture mozzarella* cheese

1 cup freshly grated *Parmesan* cheese

Torn *fresh basil leaves*, for garnish

Special Equipment: Instant read thermometer

1. Line two baking sheets with paper towels. Use a sharp knife to very thinly slice the eggplant lengthwise; try to make the slices no thicker than ⅛-inch (3mm). Place the eggplant slices on the baking sheets—it's ok if the slices overlap a bit, but don't pile them on top of each other.

2. In a colander, sprinkle the eggplant all over with 1 tablespoon of salt. Let drain in the sink for 30 minutes to 1 hour. Pat the eggplant dry with paper towels.

3. Line a baking sheet with paper towels and place it next to the stovetop.

4. Pour enough oil to come about ¼ inch (6mm) up the sides of a large, deep skillet. Heat over medium-high heat until the oil is shimmering, but not smoking, or reaches 350°F (180°C) on an instant-read thermometer.

5. In batches, without crowding, cook the eggplant, turning once, until golden and tender, 3 to 4 minutes total, and adding more oil as needed. Reduce the heat if the oil begins to smoke. Using kitchen tongs or a slotted spatula, transfer the eggplant to the paper towels.

6. Pour out all but 2 tablespoons of the oil from the skillet and heat over medium heat. Add the onions and cook, stirring often, until translucent, about 8 minutes. Stir in the garlic and cook until fragrant, 1 to 2 minutes. Add the sliced shiitake mushrooms and cook, stirring occasionally, until lightly browned, 5 to 7 minutes.

7. Pour the tomatoes, sugar, dried basil, oregano, and crushed red pepper, if using, into the skillet. Add about ¼ cup water to the tomato can and slosh it around to clean off the sides, then pour into the skillet. Season with salt and pepper. Bring to a simmer over medium heat. Reduce the heat to low and simmer, stirring occasionally, until thickened, 15 to 20 minutes. Remove from the heat.

8. Preheat the oven to 375°F (190°C). Spread a thin layer of the sauce in the bottom of a 9×13-inch (23×33cm). Layer a third of the fried eggplant slices over the sauce, and top with one-fourth of the sauce, one-fourth of the mozzarella, and one-third of the Parmesan. Repeat twice, finishing with the final quarter of mozzarella.

9. Cover loosely with aluminum foil and bake for 25 minutes. Remove the foil and bake until the cheese is bubbling and golden brown, 10 to 15 minutes more. For a browner top, turn the broiler to high for 5 minutes.

10. Let stand for 10 minutes. Top with the fresh basil leaves and serve.

159

The Best Damn ZA'ATAR
MEATBALLS *with Tagliatelle*

This isn't your conventional meatball and tomato sauce combo. In Middle Eastern cooking, meatballs are often served with lighter sauces, allowing you to really enjoy that meaty flavor. In this recipe, I serve them with a tagliatelle, but you can pair it with lots of different sides like rice or couscous. My dad loved to eat them with a nice fresh loaf of bread or baguette. Roll them into mini meatballs for an appetizer, stick them with cocktail picks, and serve with a bowl of Labneh (see page 100) on the side for dipping.

PREP: 10 minutes *COOK:* 20 minutes *TOTAL:* 30 minutes

FOR THE MEATBALLS

1½ pounds (680g) *ground beef*

½ large *white onion*, finely chopped (about 1 cup)

2 *cloves garlic*, finely minced

½ cup chopped *flat-leaf parsley* or cilantro leaves and tender stems

1 large *egg*, lightly beaten

2 tablespoons *Za'atar* (see page 98, or use store-bought), divided, plus more for sprinkling as garnish

1 teaspoon *kosher salt*

1 teaspoon *ground sumac* (see Note) or finely grated zest of 1 *lemon*

½ teaspoon *ground turmeric*

½ teaspoon *Aleppo pepper* or crushed hot red pepper (optional, see Note)

½ cup *extra-virgin olive oil*

1 tablespoon *sesame seeds* or za'atar, for sprinkling, plus more as needed

Labneh (see page 100), sprinkled with *za'atar*, for serving

Sprigs of *flat-leaf parsley*, for serving

FOR THE TAGLIATELLE

Kosher salt

1 pound (454g) *dried tagliatelle* (or long fusilli)

2 tablespoons *extra virgin olive oil*, or as needed

1 tablespoon *za'atar*

1 *lemon*, zest removed with a vegetable peeler and very thinly sliced

¼ cup chopped *parsley*

1. Preheat the oven to 375°F (190°C). In a medium bowl, using clean hands, mix the ground beef with the onion, garlic, parsley, egg, 1 tablespoon of the za'atar, salt, sumac, turmeric, and Aleppo or hot red pepper, if desired, until well combined. Shape about twelve 2-inch (5cm) meatballs and place on a baking sheet.

2. In a large oven-proof skillet, heat the oil over medium heat until it is hot and shimmering. Add the meatballs to the skillet. Increase the heat to medium-high and brown the meatballs, turning them to brown them all over, 4 to 5 minutes. Sprinkle with the sesame seeds or za'atar, adding more if necessary to cover each meatball; it's fine that some will fall off into the hot oil. Transfer the skillet to the oven and bake until crisped and cooked through, 6 to 10 minutes. Remove from the heat and cover to keep warm.

3. Bring a large pot of salted water to a boil over high heat. Add the tagliatelle and cook according to package directions until al dente. Reserve ½ cup of the pasta water. Drain the pasta and place it in a large bowl or return it to the pot. Add the olive oil and add a tablespoon of za'atar and lemon zest. Use tongs to toss to thoroughly coat. Add some pasta water or more olive oil if the pasta is too dry. Taste and add salt if needed. Sprinkle with the parsley.

4. To serve, put the labneh in a serving bowl. Sprinkle the meatballs with a garnish of za'atar or sesame seeds. Place the tagliatelle and meatballs onto plates, add a small bunch of parsley sprigs to each, and serve with the labneh.

NOTE *Aleppo pepper is a mild, fruity chile from Syria, and always sold crushed. Sumac, also always crushed, is made from the tart, dark red berries of a shrub. Both are sold at Middle Eastern grocers and online.*

Iraqi MEAT DUMPLINGS IN BEEF STEW *(Kubba Shwandar)*

These bring back such memories for me of my grandmother. She always had this dish around, and it's probably one of my absolute favorites. It takes time to prep and cook, but I can assure you most of your guests will never have eaten this dish and will fall in love. It's so hearty yet somehow still light, packed with health benefits, and has this tangy, sweet juiciness that I crave every couple of weeks. It's also really beautiful with its deep purple beet color. I'm getting hungry just writing this.

PREP: **20 minutes**   COOK: **2 hours and 20 minutes** (including chill times)

FOR THE FILLING

1 tablespoon *extra-virgin olive oil*

1 cup finely chopped *yellow onion*

1 pound (450g) *ground beef* or lamb

1 teaspoon *sweet paprika*

1 teaspoon *kosher salt*

½ teaspoon *Baharat* (see page 98)

½ teaspoon *garlic powder*

FOR THE PASTA SHELLS

2½ cups *semolina* (pasta flour), plus more for rolling

1 teaspoon *kosher salt*

3 tablespoons *extra-virgin olive oil*

FOR THE SOUP

2 tablespoons *extra-virgin olive oil*, plus more for rolling the dough

1 large *yellow onion*, diced

2 *garlic cloves*, minced

2 *celery stalks*, diced

5 medium *beets* (1 pound), peeled and diced

1× 14.5 ounce (411g) can of *crushed tomatoes*

1½ tablespoons *tomato paste*

1 tablespoon *chicken or beef bouillon paste*

3 tablespoons *sugar*

2 teaspoons *kosher salt*, plus more for serving

½ teaspoon *pepper*, plus more for serving

1 teaspoon *citric acid* (see Note)

Juice of ½ *lemon*, as needed

1. To make the filling, heat the oil in a large skillet over medium heat. Add the onion and cook, stirring, until soft and translucent, about 5 minutes. Add the lamb, paprika, salt, baharat, and garlic powder and cook, stirring occasionally and breaking up the meat with the side of a spoon, until browned, 10 to 15 minutes.

2. Drain the meat mixture in a wire sieve over the sink. Press it with a large spoon to extract as much liquid as possible. Spread on a baking sheet and freeze to cool completely, about 30 minutes.

3. Meanwhile, to make the pasta wrappers, whisk together the semolina and salt in a medium bowl. Pour in ¾ cup warm water and the oil. Use your hands to combine, then knead in the bowl for 4 to 5 minutes to form a slightly sticky but smooth dough. Tightly wrap the dough in plastic and refrigerate for 20 to 30 minutes.

4. Lightly oil a work surface. Pull off a walnut-size piece of dough and use a rolling pin to roll it out thinly into a 4-inch (10cm) round. Holding the rolled dough in one hand, place a heaping teaspoon of the filling in the center, pressing it down gently with the back of the spoon to flatten. Pinch together the edges of the dough with your fingers well to seal the filling inside, then use scissors to trim any excess dough, reserving the trimmings. Press the filled dough firmly with both hands to remove any air pockets around the filling. Gently roll the filled shell between your palms to form a smooth, slightly flattened ball. Place it on a baking sheet or platter and repeat with the remaining dough (knead the trimmings together to roll out more rounds) and filling. You should have about 30 "meatballs." Refrigerate while making the soup.

Recipe Continues

5. To make the soup, in a Dutch oven, heat the oil over medium heat. Add the onion, garlic, celery, and beets. Cook until the onion begins to soften, about 3 minutes. Stir in the tomatoes, tomato paste, bouillon paste, sugar, 2 teaspoons salt, ½ teaspoon pepper, and the citric acid. Add water to cover and bring to a boil over high heat. Reduce the heat to medium-low and cover tightly. Simmer, stirring occasionally, until the beets are tender, 45 to 50 minutes.

6. Add the "meatballs" and simmer until the semolina coating is cooked and the meat shows no sign of pink when pierced with the tip of a small sharp knife, 30 to 35 minutes. Season with salt, pepper, and lemon juice. Ladle the meatballs and stew into wide bowls and serve hot.

NOTE *Citric acid is often labeled sour salt. It adds tartness to a dish without adding liquid. You'll find it at kosher markets and online. Substitute an additional 1 tablespoon of freshly squeezed lemon juice for the citric acid in this recipe, if you wish.*

KIBBEH

Kibbeh is a great dish to serve before dinner. They're little mini footballs stuffed with a really delicious, spiced meat. They can be fried or baked to golden-brown crispiness; directions for both are given here. Serve with Tahina (see page 101).

PREP: **15 minutes**   COOK: **About 1 hour and 20 minutes (frying) and 1 hour and 45 minutes (baking) (including chill time)**

FOR THE SHELLS

2 cups *fine bulgur wheat*

1 pound (450g) *lean ground beef*

1 medium *yellow onion*, grated on the large holes of a box grater

½ cup finely chopped *flat-leaf parsley*

1 teaspoon *ground cumin*

1 teaspoon *ground allspice*

1 teaspoon *ground coriander*

1 teaspoon *kosher salt*

½ teaspoon freshly ground *black pepper*

FOR THE FILLING

1 tablespoon *extra virgin olive oil*

1 medium *yellow onion*, grated on the large holes of a box grater

1 pound (450g) *lean ground beef*

1 teaspoon *ground cinnamon*

½ teaspoon *ground cumin*

½ teaspoon *ground allspice*

½ teaspoon *dried coriander*

1 teaspoon *kosher salt*

½ teaspoon freshly ground *black pepper*

⅓ cup *pine nuts*, toasted

Vegetable oil, for frying, or extra virgin olive oil, for baking

Tahina (see page 101), sprinkled with chopped *fresh parsley* or mint, for serving

1. To prepare the shells, in a wire sieve, rinse the bulgur under cold water. Put in a bowl and add enough cold water to cover by 1 inch (2.5cm) until softened, 10 to 15 minutes. Line the sieve with a clean, thin kitchen towel or several layers of cheesecloth. Drain the bulgur, then gather the ends of the towel or cheesecloth and twist to squeeze out any excess water.

2. In a large bowl, combine the soaked bulgur, ground beef, onion, parsley, cumin, allspice, coriander, salt, and pepper. Knead the mixture thoroughly with your hands, adding a few tablespoons of ice water as needed to keep it pliable and smooth. Set aside in the refrigerator.

3. To make the filling, heat the olive oil in a skillet over medium heat. Add the onion and cook until golden, about 7 minutes. Add the ground beef, and cook, breaking up the meat with the side of a wooden spoon, until browned, about 8 minutes. Stir in the cinnamon, cumin, allspice, coriander, salt, and pepper and cook until fragrant, about 1 minute. Stir in the pine nuts. Remove from the heat and cool slightly.

4. Have ready a platter or baking sheet. Wet your hands and scoop up some of the kibbeh shell mixture and make a 2-inch (5cm) ball. Use your thumb to press a hollow center in the ball, creating a shell. Add about a tablespoon of the filling to the center, then carefully seal the opening and shape into an oval or football shape, and place on the platter. Repeat with the remaining shell and filling mixtures. Cover with plastic wrap and refrigerate for 1 hour.

5. To fry the kibbeh, line a second baking sheet with paper towels and place next to the stovetop. Pour enough vegetable oil to come about ½ inch (6mm) up the sides of a large deep skillet. Heat over medium-high heat until the oil is shimmering, but not smoking, or it reaches 350°F

(180°C) on an instant-read thermometer. In batches, without crowding, add the kibbeh to the skillet and fry, turning often with kitchen tongs, until crisp and golden brown on all sides, 5 to 6 minutes, adjusting the heat as needed to keep the oil temperature steady. Transfer to paper towels to drain. Continue with the remaining kibbeh, adding more oil to the pan if necessary.

6. To instead bake the kibbeh, preheat the oven to 400°F (200°C). Line a large baking sheet with parchment paper. Arrange the kibbeh on the prepared sheet lined with parchment paper and brush lightly with olive oil. Bake until golden brown, turning halfway through baking, turning them over halfway through baking for even browning, about 25 minutes.

7. Serve the kibbeh warm with the Tahina.

Lamb and Beef KOFTE

When it's summer outdoor cooking season, these kebabs are one of my go-to recipes—quick, easy, and always a hit. Grill up some veggies of your choice as a side. The seasoning is so much more interesting than a regular burger! Insider tip: The touch of baking soda helps the mixture stick together and stay securely on the skewers (you're welcome!). Be sure to allow at least 30 minutes of refrigeration so the kofte can firm up before grilling.

PREP: 20 minutes   *COOK:* 16 to 18 minutes
(chill time of 1 to 12 hours)   *TOTAL:* About 1 hour and 40 minutes or more

1 large *yellow onion*, cut into chunks

4 *cloves garlic*

1½ cups *flat-leaf parsley* leaves and tender stems

1 pound (454g) *ground lamb*

1 pound (454g) *ground beef*

2 slices *soft bread*

2½ teaspoons *kosher salt*

1 teaspoon *sweet paprika*

½ teaspoon *ground cumin*

½ teaspoon freshly ground *black pepper*

½ teaspoon *baking soda*

Vegetable oil, for coating

Flaky salt, for garnish

FOR SERVING

1 small *red onion*, cut into wedges

3 *plum tomatoes*, cut into wedges

Extra virgin olive oil, as needed

12 sprigs *flat-leaf parsley*

Tahina (see page 101) or Hummus (see page 99)

Flatbread, such as laffa pita, warmed

Special Equipment: Food processor, 6 to 8 flat metal skewers (or 12 to 16 bamboo skewers, soaked in water for 30 minutes)

1. In the bowl of a food processor, pulse the onion, garlic, and parsley until minced, scraping down the sides as needed. (Or, using a large, sharp knife, finely chop the ingredients and transfer to a large bowl.)

2. Break up the ground lamb and ground beef and add them to the food processor, along with the bread, salt, paprika, cumin, pepper, and baking soda, and pulse a few times until just combined. (Or add the ingredients to the vegetables in the bowl and mix well.) Do not overmix, as overworking can make the kofte tough.

3. Line a baking sheet or platter with plastic wrap. Wet your hands and divide the meat into 10 equal portions. Mold each portion around a skewer, pressing to form an elongated oval or cylindrical shape along the length of the skewer—basically, like a corndog. (If using soaked bamboo skewers, place 2 skewers parallel to each other before adding the meat and shaping.) Place on the baking sheet or platter. Repeat with the remaining mixture and skewers. Cover with plastic wrap and refrigerate for at least 1 hour or up to 12 hours to firm up.

4. To grill the kofte, preheat a gas grill on medium-high, about 500°F (260°C). Brush the grates clean. Lightly brush the kofte with oil. Place the skewers on the grill, perpendicular to the grid, and cover. Cook, until the underside is charred, 8 to 9 minutes. Carefully turn the kofte and char the other side, 8 to 9 minutes more.

5. To broil the kofte, position a broiler rack 6 inches (15cm) from the heat source and preheat the broiler on high. Line a baking sheet with aluminum foil and lightly grease the foil with oil. Arrange the skewers on the sheet and broil until browned and cooked through, turning after about 8 minutes, 16 to 18 minutes total.

6. Transfer the skewers to a platter and sprinkle them with flaky salt. Surround them with the red onion and tomatoes. Drizzle with olive oil and add the parsley. Serve immediately with tahina and the laffa on the side.

BAMYA
(Beef and Okra Stew)

Bamya means "okra" in Arabic and it's the starring vegetable in this flavorful stew. This was another one of Grandma Saida's dishes in rotation. I know that okra can be a controversial vegetable, so if it isn't a favorite of yours, Grandma always had a solution for that and would make it with green beans. Kid friendly too! Simple white basmati rice does the trick as its pairing.

PREP: **10 minutes**   _COOK:_ **About 2 hours and 25 minutes**

1 pound (450g) *beef chuck*, cut into 1-inch (2.5cm) cubes

Kosher salt and freshly ground *black pepper*

3 tablespoons *extra-virgin olive oil*, divided

1 large *yellow onion*, finely chopped

4 *cloves garlic*, minced

1 teaspoon *ground coriander*

1 teaspoon *ground cumin*

½ teaspoon *sweet paprika*

½ teaspoon *ground cinnamon*

½ teaspoon *ground allspice*

2 tablespoons *tomato paste*

1× 14.5 ounce (411g) can of *diced tomatoes*, with juices, or 2 cups chopped ripe fresh tomatoes

1 tablespoon *beef bouillon paste*

1 pound fresh or frozen *okra*, tops and tips trimmed if fresh, sliced ½-inch (12mm) thick

Juice of 1 *lemon*, or as needed

Chopped *flat-leaf parsley* or cilantro, for garnish

FOR SERVING
Cooked basmati rice

Lemon wedges

Flatbread, such as laffa

1. Season the beef with 1 teaspoon salt and ½ teaspoon black pepper. In a large Dutch oven, heat 2 tablespoons of the oil over medium-high heat. In batches without crowding, add the beef and cook, turning occasionally, until browned, about 8 minutes. Using a slotted spoon, transfer the beef to a plate.

2. Add the remaining 1 tablespoon oil to the pot, then add the chopped onion and cook until translucent, about 7 minutes. Stir in the garlic, coriander, cumin, paprika, cinnamon, and allspice and cook, stirring occasionally, until fragrant, about 1 minute.

3. Stir in the tomato paste and cook until a little darker in color, 1 to 2 minutes. Stir in the tomatoes and their juices and bring to a simmer. Stir in 3 cups of water and the bouillon paste.

4. Return the beef and its juices to the pot and bring to a boil. Reduce the heat to medium-low, cover tightly, and simmer until the beef is tender, about 1½ hours to 2½ hours (the longer the better).

5. Stir in the okra and season with salt and pepper. Cover and simmer until the okra is tender but not falling apart, 5 to 10 minutes. Stir in 1 tablespoon lemon juice or to taste and simmer for a minute more. Season with salt and pepper.

6. Sprinkle with the parsley or cilantro. Spoon over rice in deep bowls. Serve with the lemon wedges and flatbread on the side.

Aunt Elaine's STUFFED ARTICHOKES

Auntie Elaine, my late father-in-law's sister, always wows guests with this aesthetically pleasing and absolutely delish stuffed artichoke dish. You can swap the beef for ground lamb or mix beef with lamb. It's a great party dish because everyone can grab a serving for themselves.

PREP: 15 minutes   *COOK:* 1 hour

FOR THE STUFFING

1 medium *yellow onion*, peeled and halved

3 *celery stalks*, coarsely grated

1 medium *baking potato*, peeled

1 pound (450g) *ground beef*

¼ cup chopped *flat-leaf parsley* leaves and thin stems

¼ cup chopped *fresh dill*

2 teaspoons *kosher salt*

½ teaspoon freshly ground *black pepper*

1 teaspoon *sweet paprika*

½ teaspoon *curry powder*

4× 14-ounce (400g) cans of [medium, large, or extra-large] *artichoke bottoms*, drained, patted dry

Neutral *vegetable oil*, for frying

FOR THE SAUCE

⅓ cup *extra-virgin olive oil*

3 *cloves garlic*, minced

½ teaspoon *kosher salt*

Chopped *flat-leaf parsley*, for garnish

Mom's Basmati Rice with Lima Beans and Dill (see page 150) or basmati rice, for serving

Special Equipment: Food processor, Instant-read thermometer

1. Preheat the oven to 350°F (180°C)

2. For the filling, pulse the onion, celery, and potato in a food processor until finely chopped (or use a box grater). Transfer the mixture to a wire sieve strainer and press gently to drain any excess liquid. Transfer to a large bowl.

3. Add the ground beef, parsley, dill, salt, pepper, paprika, and curry powder to the bowl. Using your hands, mix everything together until well combined.

4. For each artichoke bottom, scoop up a portion of the filling, place in the artichoke, and mound into a dome. Place on a baking sheet or platter.

5. Line a baking sheet with a wire rack and place next to the stovetop. Pour enough vegetable oil into a large, deep skillet to come about ½-inch (12mm) up the sides. Heat over medium heat until the oil is hot and shimmering but not smoking, or 350°F (180°C) on an instant-read thermometer.

6. In batches so as not to crowd them, add a few artichokes, meat-side down, and fry until browned, 2 to 3 minutes. Use a metal spatula, if necessary, to loosen them from the bottom of the pan, then flip and cook for 2 to 3 minutes on the other side. Carefully transfer the artichokes to the baking sheet.

7. Bake the artichokes for 15 to 20 minutes until they're golden and crisp on top.

8. While the artichokes are baking, make the sauce. Add the olive oil to a medium pan set over medium-low heat. Add the garlic cloves and salt and saute until fragrant. Set aside.

9. Remove the artichokes from the oven and transfer them to a serving platter. Spoon the sauce over and around the artichokes. Sprinkle with the parsley and serve with the rice.

MOVE IT!

Space planning for your party is a must. I've seen many parties where a small apartment has made the party even more intimate and enjoyable because of the guests' proximity to each other. In fact, we all remember the dark days of the pandemic when we couldn't socialize at all, much less sit or stand next to each other. Now that those times are over, close quarters at a party are actually welcome, at least in my home. Even in big spaces, there is a way to make it feel intimate.

LOOK AROUND your space for areas to make into easy and cozy mingling spaces for your guests. If needed, rearrange a small table with a few chairs, and you're good to go. People sitting snugly together encourages connection, and that's what we want to accomplish here. If you have a fireplace, light it and make that a different area of mingling as well. When making your conversation nooks, don't forget to enhance the area with candles and flowers which also serves as an indicator, a sign so to speak that says "sit here!" Make each area cozy and inviting, luring your guests in.

I think every good host should own an inexpensive portable table or two stored away until needed. With the right tablecloth, no one will be able to spot it. When it comes to seating, folding chairs are indispensable. But in this case, don't be too thrifty because no one likes sitting on a rickety chair with a hard bottom. My portable chairs have cushions, and it's worth it for my guest's (and usually my own) comfort.

DON'T BE AFRAID to move furniture out to make the flow feel more fluid. If a big couch lives in the middle of the room and interrupts traffic, move it against a wall or have someone push it into another room. Think out of the box when hosting. It's okay to move things around in your home to throw a great gathering.

When I have a big dinner with lots of people (which as you can infer, happens often), sometimes instead of making one long table, I'll choose to set the second one perpendicular to the first, as it makes for a friendlier, more united atmosphere. Find a separate place for the kid's table, as they tend to wander off quickly and don't need to use up your table real estate if it's tight. That being said, it depends on the age and the kid. Levi always has a spot at our big dinner table because A. he would be very insulted if he wasn't with the teens and B. nobody enjoys food and talking about the food more than he does! If the kids are on the young side, you can provide something to keep them busy and maybe quieter, like coloring books and paper plane napkins. (At Thanksgiving, I set them up in a separate area with pumpkins and paint and let them decorate for festive pieces while eating their meals.)

Just like the other aspects of your party, let your creativity flow and don't be afraid to temporarily redecorate your space. You can always put things back when your guests leave.

5

CHEERS!

COCKTAILS *are part of the* NEW YORK LEGEND.

How many old movies take place in my fabulous city with the elegant, well-dressed characters sipping an ice-cold martini? FYI, I am currently pregnant while writing this, salivating over the idea of an ice-cold martini! When not with child, I do my part to keep the image and tradition alive. I even created a brand to continue cocktail culture (without the additives).

My friends, however, have varying tastes in their beverages of choice, and as a good host, it's my job to be sure that everyone has something they like to drink. I have two suggestions that work well. First, choose cocktail recipes that are adaptable for different kinds of liquor. It's no secret that I have my own mezcal brand, Mezcalum, so of course I lean toward that Mexican spirit, especially since I feel much better the day after when I stick to it. But a Mezcalum Negroni (see page 190) can just as easily be made with vodka or bourbon or gin.

My second suggestion is to set up stations for each liquor or cocktail. This is super fun and looks great! You might want to print out a recipe card or two to help the people who are challenged in their mixology skills. I'll put a bottle of the chosen liquor(s) for the table, with the appropriate juices, mixers, and garnishes for a specific cocktail. Don't forget the glasses, stirrers, and a filled ice bucket. A jigger will come in handy if the guests care to measure the ingredients (plus, I love how they look). Now, let everyone play. It's an adult version of finger painting, where creativity can run rampant. The recipes are there for people who want them. You'll see exactly what I mean with the recipes in this chapter, which are often designed for the station concept.

Top-notch mixers and garnishes are easy ways to elevate your cocktails. Instead of small Spanish-stuffed olives, put out a ramekin full of colossal, pimiento-filled olives, some stuffed with fresh blue cheese (see page 194), already speared with a toothpick (the bamboo or metal ones are nice), ready to add to the martinis. As I describe on page 194, offer a large spread of garnishes beyond celery sticks for your Bloody Marias. When a drink calls for fruit juice, use fresh whenever you can. Serve high-quality individual bottles of tonic and sparkling water, not just from a generic plastic liter jug (and as a rule at home I actually do not buy anything in plastic because it's bad for the environment AND for you!)

I do have some friends who don't drink alcohol (I'm currently that friend). There will be fruit juices for many of the cocktails—grapefruit for Palomas (see page 185), cranberry or pomegranate for Cosmos (see page 196), lime for the Mexcalitas. So, I invite the non-drinkers to make fresh fruit spritzers with their favorite juice, as I always have a good sparkling water (I like San Pellegrino) in the house, or just follow the recipe cards and make a fabulous mocktail (see page 200).

Be sure there is plenty of chilled white wine and beer in the fridge for their fans and have a bottle of red wine handy for after dinner. If you're anything like me, chill your red a bit too. If you have a wine fridge set white and red at the appropriate temps but if not, just stick a bottle of red in the fridge like 30 minutes before serving. Does the trick! You're all set for a first-class cocktail party for the books (or movies).

MAXIMILIAN AFFAIR

This is one of my most treasured recent discoveries. The history of the cocktail and its name is fascinating and beautiful, blending a Mexican and French spirit from a story about an old historic battle. Not to mention, there's something about the elegant, unique shape of a martini glass that puts you in the mood to sip and savor. It's the perfect vessel for this complex drink with smoky, floral, and bittersweet flavors. The finishing touch is a twist of lemon peel. Make sure you *really* twist the zest over the drink so the citrus oils float on the surface.

PREP: **5 minutes**

1½ fluid ounces **mezcal**, such as Mezcalum

1 fluid ounce **elderflower liqueur**, such as St-Germain

½ fluid ounce **sweet vermouth**

¼ fluid ounce freshly squeezed **lemon juice**

Ice cubes, for shaking

Lemon zest twist, (remove from the lemon with a vegetable peeler or zester), for garnish

Special Equipment: Cocktail shaker and strainer, Martini glass (chilled)

1. Fill a cocktail shaker with ice. Pour in the mezcal, elderflower liqueur, sweet vermouth, and lemon juice. Close the shaker and shake vigorously for 15 seconds, or until the shaker feels cold to the touch.

2. Strain the cocktail into a chilled martini glass. Literally twist the lemon zest over the drink. Drop the twist into the glass. Serve.

MEASURING COCKTAILS

Every mixologist measures the cocktail ingredients with a jigger, so the results are always the same. Don't let the fluid ounces measurement throw you off. I encourage you to use a jigger, but all you really need to know is that 1 fluid ounce = 2 tablespoons. If you see ½ fluid ounce, that would be 1 tablespoon, and 2 fluid ounces would be 4 tablespoons. Easy! So, even if you don't have a jigger (and I hope you run out and get one, if you don't), you have the info to get your cocktail party started like a pro.

Classic PALOMA

This one's a go-to for all Mezcalum employees (myself included). Salt and grapefruit are old friends (if you've ever had a Salty Dog, you know the drill), and the salted rim and the use of our lightly smoky mezcal bring the old south-of-the-border cocktail into the 21st century. If you don't have fresh grapefruit, you can swap for grapefruit soda. I love using Fever Tree and Jarritos brands especially.

PREP: **10 minutes**

Kosher salt, for the glass

1 thin wedge *grapefruit* or lime, for the glass

2 fluid ounces *mezcal*, such as Mezcalum or silver tequila

½ fluid ounce freshly squeezed *lime juice*

Grapefruit soda, chilled, as needed

Ice cubes, for serving and shaking

Grapefruit slice and *lime wheel*, for garnish

Special equipment: Cocktail shaker and strainer, rocks glass

1. Pour a few tablespoons of kosher salt on a small plate. Rub the flesh side of the grapefruit or lime wedge along the outer edge of the lip of the rocks glass. Holding the glass at an angle, roll the moistened outer edge of the glass in the salt. Try not to get any salt on the inside lip or in the glass. (If you do, just shake it out.) Fill the glass with ice.

2. Fill a cocktail shaker with ice. Pour in the mezcal or tequila and lime juice. Close the shaker and shake vigorously for 15 seconds, or until the shaker feels cold to the touch.

3. Strain the mezcal or tequila and lime mixture into the prepared glass. Pour in enough grapefruit soda to fill the glass. Garnish with a slice of grapefruit and a lime wheel and serve.

Espresso MARTINI

If you opt for Mezcalum, it will set this martini apart from the crowd, giving it an earthy undertone that complements the roasted taste of the coffee. The double-straining guarantees a silky-smooth finish, free of ice chips and coffee grounds. Coffee beans are the traditional garnish for this invigorating cocktail. This is my go-to with friends or Abe before a night out (or for dessert).

PREP: **5 minutes**

2 fluid ounces *vodka* or *mezcal*, such as Mezcalum

1 fluid ounce freshly brewed *espresso* (see Note)

½ fluid ounce *coffee liqueur*

¼ fluid ounce *agave syrup*

Ice cubes, for shaking

3 *whole coffee beans*, for garnish

Special Equipment: Cocktail shaker, Small fine-mesh wire strainer, Martini glass (chilled)

1. Fill a cocktail shaker with ice. Pour in the vodka or mezcal, espresso, coffee liqueur and agave syrup. Close the shaker and shake vigorously for 15 seconds, or until the shaker feels cold to the touch.

2. Using a Hawthorne strainer with the shaker container, strain the drink through a small, fine-mesh strainer into your chilled martini glass. This is called double-straining. Float the coffee beans on top as a garnish. Serve.

NOTE *Use your favorite method for brewing the espresso—pod machine, Moka pot, or even a cup from your local coffee stand because the espresso can be cold for this recipe. Instant espresso is not the best option here.*

Spicy MEZCALITA

A Mezcalita is a margarita that has decided to make slightly different choices. It gets a spiced glass rim with Tajín, a sweet-and-tangy seasoning. It was inspired from a recipe by Brittany Criss (@brittsbevs), a budding cocktail creator. Your choice of orange liqueur will affect the color and flavor of your drink—triple sec lends a more traditional vibe and dark/brandy-based Grand Marnier will lean sweeter—but both types are good! I personally like Magdala Orange Liqueur. If you can find it, it adds a delicate sweetness that's both light and casual while still adding that orange sweet citrus undertone you need.

PREP: **10 minutes**

Chile-lime seasoning, such as Tajín, for the glass

3 fluid ounces **mezcal**, such as Mezcalum

1½ fluid ounces **orange liqueur**, such as triple sec (Cointreau) or Grand Mariner

¾ fluid ounce fresh **lime juice**

½ fluid ounce **dark agave syrup**

Ice, for serving and shaking

Orange wheel and **lime wheel**, for garnish

Special Equipment: Cocktail shaker and strainer, Rocks glass, 6-inch (15cm) bamboo or metal skewer

1. Using a pastry brush, starting at the outside lip of a rocks glass, brush a horizontal swath of the chamoy, about 3 inches (7.5cm) wide and long. Sprinkle the chamoy with the chili-lime seasoning, trying not to get any seasoning inside the glass. (If you do, shake it out.). Fill the glass with ice.

2. Fill a cocktail shaker with ice and pour in the mezcal, orange liqueur, lime juice, and agave syrup. Close the shaker and shake vigorously for 15 seconds, or until the shaker feels cold to the touch. Pour the drink into the prepared glass.

3. Place the lime wheel on top of the orange wheel and horizontally thread a 6-inch (15cm) skewer through them to secure together. Garnish the drink with the citrus wheel and serve.

NEGRONI

The first Negroni was invented about a hundred years ago in Florence by a bartender for Count Negroni. The story literally makes me like the cocktail even more, if that was possible. The combination of floral and bitter proved to be a smash hit. It was soon discovered that other liquor could be swapped for the gin with success, and my vote is for mezcal. (Although if you use bourbon or rye, it's called a Boulevardier.) Few drinks quench your thirst on a hot summer day like the Negroni.

PREP: **5 minutes**

1 fluid ounce *gin* or mezcal, such as Mezcalum

1 fluid ounce *Campari*

1 fluid ounce *sweet vermouth*

Ice, for serving and mixing

Orange zest twist, for garnish

Special Equipment: Cocktail shaker and strainer, Rocks glass

1. Fill a rocks glass with ice.

2. Fill a cocktail shaker with ice. Pour in the gin or mezcal, Campari, and sweet vermouth. Stir until well chilled.

3. Strain into the rocks glass. Literally twist the orange zest over the drink. Drop the twist into the glass. Serve.

Ultimate DIRTY MARTINI
with Blue Cheese Olives

I hardly ever drink vodka as it's my kryptonite, but I love a good vodka martini with blue cheese olives. It's all I longed for while pregnant. With the popularity of the vodka martini, a lot of people forget that the OG version is with gin. This is the ultimate recipe featuring a double-dirty dose of olives, brine, and stuffed with blue cheese. You can find the olives in well-stocked markets and liquor stores, but why not make your own? The Dirty Martini station is always one of the most crowded at my parties.

PREP: **40 minutes (including chill time)**

FOR THE BLUE CHEESE OLIVES

1× 13.5oz (350g) jar large *green olives* packed in brine (reserve the brine)

½ cup crumbled *blue cheese*, softened

2 tablespoons *cream cheese*, softened

⅛ teaspoon *garlic powder*

⅛ teaspoon freshly ground *black pepper*

⅛ teaspoon *smoked paprika* (optional)

FOR THE MARTINI

3 fluid ounces *vodka* or gin

1 fluid ounce *reserved brine* from the olive jar

¼ fluid ounce *dry vermouth*

3 *blue-cheese olives*, for garnish

Special Equipment: Cocktail shaker and strainer, Martini glass (chilled)

1. To make the blue-cheese olives, drain the olives well, reserving the brine (you'll need it to make the martini dirty!). Pat the olives dry with paper towels.

2. In a small bowl, using a fork, mash the blue cheese and cream cheeses, garlic powder, black pepper, and smoked paprika, if using, until blended. Scoop the cheese mixture into a small ziplock bag. Snip off a small corner of the bag to make a hole. Gently pipe the cheese mixture into each olive, completely filling the cavity. Place on a plate or tray. Cover with plastic wrap and refrigerate for at least 30 minutes to firm up the filling. (The olives can be refrigerated for up to 1 week.)

3. Fill a cocktail shaker with ice. Pour in the vodka or gin, olive brine, and vermouth. Close the shaker and shake vigorously for 15 seconds, or until the shaker feels cold to the touch.

4. Strain the drink into the martini glass. Thread the olives on a cocktail pick and add to the martini. Serve.

BLOODY MARIAS

I love this drink so much because it gives my guests a chance to play with garnishes and load up the glass. It's usually the pre-brunch drink of choice when friends come early and hungry before all the food is out and ready to be served. I like to call it the belly warmer station. Make a big pitcher (with ice on the side), serve with mezcal, an array of the add-ons, and let everyone get creative! This is one of my favorite drinks for a cocktail station. I always put out a good bottle of vodka, too.

PREP: **30 minutes**

FOR THE BLOODY MARIA MIX

1 quart (1L) *tomato juice*

½ cup freshly squeezed *lemon juice*

2 tablespoons *prepared horseradish*, or more to taste

1 tablespoon *Worcestershire sauce*

1 tablespoon *Tabasco*

1 teaspoon *celery salt*

1 teaspoon freshly ground *black pepper*

24 fluid ounces (3 cups) *mezcal*, such as Mezcalum or vodka

FOR THE GARNISHES

Blue Cheese Olives (see page 193)

Celery sticks

Cucumber spears

Thick-cut bacon, cooked and threaded on cocktail picks (see Note)

Hard-boiled egg halves

Cooked shrimp, peeled, with tail segment attached (optional)

Cornichons

Small pickled vegetables such as banana pepper rings, pearl onions, asparagus tips, okra, baby corn, or whatever you like

Cubed firm *feta*

Lemon wedges

Ice cubes, for serving

Special Equipment: 8 rocks or highball glasses, Cocktail stirrers

1. To make the Bloody Maria mix, in a large pitcher with a tight-fitting lid, add the tomato juice, lemon juice, 2 tablespoons of the horseradish, Worcestershire sauce, Tabasco, celery salt, and pepper. Close the pitcher and shake vigorously to combine. (If your pitcher doesn't have a lid, whisk the ingredients together well.) Taste and add more horseradish for a spicier kick. (The mix can be refrigerated for up to 1 day.)

2. To prepare the garnishes, put each one in its own bowl and arrange at your serving station. Put out the glasses, a filled ice bucket, and cocktail stirrers.

3. For each drink, fill a rocks or highball glass with ice. Fill the glass ⅓ with mezcal and top it off with the Bloody Maria mix. Stir to mix with a cocktail stirrer.

4. Invite guests to take as much or as little from the garnish station as they'd like—or that their glass will hold!

NOTE *For the bacon garnish, weave each strip onto a bamboo skewer. Place on a microwave-safe plate lined with a double thickness of paper towels. Microwave according to the package directions until crisp and browned. Transfer to fresh paper towels to drain and cool.*

Deuxmoi's POMEGRANATE COSMOPOLITAN

I know that everyone loves a good Cosmo, but maybe it's time for a little makeover? I'm thinking . . . why not pomegranate juice, with a similar red color and tart flavor profile as cranberry? A bonus is that pomegranate juice is usually sold unsweetened, so you can adjust the sweetness with agave.

<u>PREP:</u> **5 minutes**

2 fluid ounces *vodka*

1 fluid ounce *triple sec*, such as Cointreau

1 fluid ounce *unsweetened pomegranate juice*

½ fluid ounce freshly squeezed *lime juice*

½ fluid ounce *agave syrup* (optional)

Ice, for shaking

Pomegranate seeds, for garnish (optional)

Orange or *lime twist*, for garnish

Special equipment: Cocktail shaker and strainer, martini glass (chilled)

1. Fill a cocktail shaker with ice. Pour in the vodka, triple sec, pomegranate juice, lime juice, and agave syrup, if using. Close the shaker and shake vigorously for 15 seconds, or until the shaker feels cold to the touch.

2. Strain the mixture into a chilled martini glass. Add a few pomegranate seeds, if using, and perch an orange or lime twist on the rim. Serve.

MAKES

1

cocktail

The MEXICAN 75

You may have had a French 75, a gin and Champagne cocktail that gets its name from a French-American field gun in WWI that packed quite a punch . . . as the drink will do if you aren't careful. Here is my version with mezcal because you know I love a Mexican-French affair (see the Maximilian Affair on page 182).

PREP: **5 minutes**

2 fluid ounces *mezcal*, such as Mezcalum

¾ fluid ounce *agave syrup*

¾ fluid ounce fresh *lime juice*

Champagne, chilled, for topping off

Lime wheel, for garnish

Special Equipment: Cocktail shaker, Cocktail strainer, Coupe glass

1. Fill a cocktail shaker with ice. Pour in the mezcal, agave, and lime juice. Close the shaker and shake vigorously for 15 seconds, or until the shaker feels cold to the touch.

2. Strain the mixture into a coupe glass and fill to the top with Champagne. Perch the lime wheel on the rim. Serve.

Immuno MOCKTAIL

I really love this drink. It's so healthy, delicious, and refreshing, and we love to make this at home when we're feeling run down. It's even good warmed up and is a great option for a mocktail. You could actually turn this into a cocktail with your favorite spirit if you wanted.

PREP: **5 minutes**

2 fluid ounces freshly squeezed *orange juice*

1 fluid ounce *elderberry syrup*

½ fluid ounce freshly squeezed *lemon juice*

¼ teaspoon *ground turmeric*, or more to taste

Sparkling water

Orange slice, for garnish

Special Equipment: Cocktail shaker, Cocktail straine, Rocks or highball glass

1. Combine the orange juice, elderberry syrup, lemon juice, and turmeric in a cocktail shaker. Fill the shaker ¾ full with ice. Close the shaker and shake vigorously for 15 seconds, or until the shaker feels cold to the touch.

2. Strain the drink into a rocks or highball glass filled with ice. (Alternatively, for a layered look, shake the citrus juices and turmeric and strain into a glass filled with crushed ice. Drizzle the elderberry syrup over the ice.)

3. Top off with sparkling water and garnish with an orange slice, if desired.

SHAKEN OR STIRRED?

Your bar gear should be an indicator of your personal style and not be hidden in a cabinet. In my opinion, every host needs a good-looking cocktail kit, with a shaker, jigger, strainer, and bar spoon. Styles range from Art Deco to mid-century retro to modern. Choose a set that complements your taste.

Some shakers have built-in pourers, which eliminates the need for a strainer, but the base container is indispensable for shaking or stirring. The agitation of shaking or stirring dilutes the ice a bit to balance the strength of the alcohol, making a better cocktail, as well as ensuring that icy, perfect temperature.

TRUST ME ON THIS
If your shaker doesn't include a spout, use a strainer to pour the drink into its glass. A Hawthorne strainer is the basic perforated cup-like tool and holds back the ice. Sometimes the cocktail is double-strained through a fine mesh sieve to remove any bubbles.

ICE BUCKETS AND TONGS
are even more opportunities to add to your décor. If purchasing, consider an insulated model that not only looks good, but guarantees to keep the cubes frozen for a long time so you aren't constantly replacing melted ice. I have both my pretty ice bucket and my functional insulated one. Antique models look great but often lack this feature. But I still love to search for old barware that tells a story. Ice trays are another seemingly mundane item that can be improved upon. Your guests who like their drinks "on the rocks" will love it if you serve their favorite liquor in a big glass with a huge, single ice cube that doesn't melt too quickly. You can even get them customized for special events. So fun!

You'll see that drink recipes are measured in fluid ounces, not tablespoons. For that reason, be sure to have a jigger with the ounces clearly marked. Measuring correctly means that your drinks will be deliciously consistent every time you make them. Until you have a jigger, know that 1 ounce equals 2 tablespoons, and fake it.

COCKTAIL GLASSWARE
is another level of eye candy and a world unto itself. Think about the kind of cocktails you and your friends like and start with the glasses that match those favorites. Old-fashioneds, collins (an old word for tall drinks like gin and tonics), or martinis all have their specific glasses. But your crowd may prefer wine or beer. And, to get technical, there are even glasses for each specific kind of beer (such as lager) or wine (cabernet vs. Beaujolais), but one for each could drive you crazy. Have fun picking the glasses that suit your style, and your needs (for example, I'm a big Bourdeaux fan, so I have Bordeaux-specific glassware). Many glasses have versatile uses. Martini glasses can even hold desserts (malabi could be so cute in a martini glass!).

COCKTAIL NAPKINS
are a must-have that, nonetheless, are easy to forget. Napkins and coasters are another extension of your personal style and taste, so choose them carefully. If you entertain as often as I do, you may want to buy napkins in bulk, so you never run out unexpectedly. I also invested in a nice stone cocktail napkin holder. Cloth cocktail napkins, even though they are high maintenance, are another way to pump up the elegance factor of your party. I only use mine for special occasions.

6

DESSERTS

If you've ever BEEN TO *a* JEWISH WEDDING

or bar/bat mitzvah, you have undoubtedly encountered the edible miracle of The Dessert Table, an awesome array of virtually every dessert under the sun. When I was a kid, you couldn't walk on upper Broadway without being tempted (and giving in) to an array of desserts in the store windows. Not to mention the shops that sold sweets that weren't baked. Penny candy stores, fancy chocolate shops, mom-and-pop stores that sold only nuts and dried fruits, ice cream stores, shops that only sold chocolate chip cookies. There were bakeries that specialized in desserts from the old country—babka, strudel, and of course, bagels (okay, not sweet unless you got cinnamon-raisin). The walk from 72nd to 86th streets was like a dessert table come to life. It is only slightly different now, with vegan ice cream shops and bakeries replacing the OG versions.

These days, I pay homage to these sweet treats with what I make for my parties. But I focus more on the desserts from our family's Cuban and Israeli heritage. I'm especially fond of the pistachio desserts that remind me of my Yemenite relatives and their fresh-from-the-oven Baklavas (see page 218), knafeh, and Butter Cookies (see page 216), baked goods that fill my kitchen with buttery aromas. Abe's family is represented by cool and creamier treats like Flan (see page 211) and tres leches cake.

Coffee cakes, the lighter and fluffier the better, have always been my Kryptonite. To that end, I offer two sure-fire winners: Marble Cake (see page 227) and Poppy Seed (see page 224). How could anyone choose between this duo? I encourage you to have a nonstick fluted tube (a.k.a. Bundt) pan for these beauties. This kind of cake is relatively easy to make, and it has many advantages over competitors. It doesn't need frosting and it's good with just a dusting of powdered sugar. It can be eaten out of hand (here's your after-school snack, kids). And it makes a lot of servings. What's not to love?

When it's time for a party, it's fun to recreate the Dessert Table feeling with bites and small slices of many different sweets. Just like I will keep snacks out towards the end of a brunch or dinner party, I will bring out new desserts when the party seems like it's winding down. If it's someone's birthday and I'm serving up a gooey layer cake (or Jenna's Pavlova [see page 214]), I will put out plates and forks. But most of the time, I regard desserts as finger food to encourage lots of small tastes—mini pastries, bite-sized brownies, cookies, and so on.

Have a spread of sweets that will make the most dedicated dieter submit.

Dulce de Leche NO-CHURN ICE CREAM

Homemade ice cream is probably the ultimate summer dessert. I learned how to make this simple version that doesn't require an ice cream machine, and now I'm in big trouble, as it's too easy to have ice cream in the freezer all the time. As a nod to Abe's Cuban heritage, I like the dulce de leche flavoring, and my kids are also obsessed. A simple sprinkle of kosher salt gives this a salted caramel flavor.

PREP: **15 minutes**   *FREEZING:* **At least 6 hours**

2 cups cold **heavy whipping cream**

1× 14-ounce (387g) can **sweetened condensed milk**

1× 13.4-ounce (380g) can **dulce de leche**, divided

1 teaspoon **vanilla extract**

Pinch of **kosher salt**

Flaky sea salt (optional)

Special Equipment: Electric hand mixer, 9×5-inch (23×12.5cm) metal loaf pan

1. In a chilled large bowl, whip the heavy cream with an electric mixer on high speed until stiff peaks form. Set aside. In a medium bowl, whisk the sweetened condensed milk, a scant half of the dulce de leche (½ cup), vanilla extract, and salt until smooth and well combined.

2. Using a spatula, in three additions, gently fold the whipped cream into the dulce de leche mixture, keeping the mixture light and airy. Pour half of the ice cream mixture into the loaf pan.

3. Drizzle half of the remaining dulce de leche over the top and gently swirl it using a knife or spoon. Add the rest of the ice cream mixture on top, then drizzle and swirl the remaining dulce de leche for a marbled effect.

4. Cover tightly with plastic wrap and freeze until firm, at least 6 hours or overnight.

5. Scoop and serve. Sprinkle each serving with a pinch of flaky sea salt, if desired.

Abe's Favorite
CUBAN-STYLE FLAN

I feel like every country has a recipe for custard, and this is the Cuban version. I had to learn this because of how much Abe loves and craves it. It gets its silky-smooth texture from a combination of canned milks and extra egg yolks. For even cooking that gives the best consistency, the flan is baked in a pan of hot water. Instead of experimenting with restaurant-y flavors, our family prefers the old-fashioned vanilla version. Remember... this is a make-ahead recipe and must be well chilled for at least a few hours before unmolding. Abe the babe loves when I make this for him on his birthday!

PREP: 10 minutes   *COOK:* 5 hours and 15 minutes (including chill time)

FOR THE CARAMEL
1 cup *granulated sugar*

FOR THE CUSTARD
2 large *eggs*

3 large *egg yolks*

1× 14-ounce (354g) can *sweetened condensed milk*

1× 12-ounce (396g) can *evaporated milk*

1 tbsp *vanilla extract*

Special Equipment: 9-inch (23cm) round heatproof baking dish or metal cake pan, Roasting pan for water bath

1. To prepare the caramel, add the sugar to a small saucepan. Add ¼ cup water and stir over medium-high heat until boiling and the sugar has dissolved. Stop stirring and simmer until the caramel is deep amber and lightly smoking, about 5 minutes. (Don't undercook the caramel—judge by the color, not by the timing.) Immediately pour into a 9-inch (23cm) round cake pan or baking dish, tilting the dish to coat the bottom evenly. Set aside for the caramel to set.

2. Preheat the oven to 350°F (180°C). In a large bowl, whisk the whole eggs and egg yolks together until combined. Add the sweetened condensed milk, evaporated milk, 1 cup water, and the vanilla. Mix until combined.

3. Place the caramel-coated pan in a larger roasting pan. Pour the custard mixture through a fine-mesh wire sieve directly into the pan. (This removes the tiny white cords on the egg yolks.) Cover tightly with aluminum foil. Pour in enough hot tap water to come halfway up the sides of the cake pan.

4. Bake until the flan is set but still slightly jiggly in the center when gently shaken, 50 to 60 minutes. (You have to remove the foil to do this—be careful of any steam.)

5. Remove the setup from the oven and let it cool in the water bath for about 15 minutes. Transfer the flan pan to a wire rack to cool completely. Refrigerate, covered, until chilled, at least 4 hours. (The flan can be refrigerated for up to 2 days.)

6. To unmold, run a knife along the edges of the flan to loosen it. Place a serving plate with a lip over the baking dish and quickly invert it, letting the caramel sauce flow over the top. Cut into wedges and serve chilled.

Mini MALABIS

Pudding is one of the most comforting of desserts, and this Middle Eastern recipe brings back memories of childhood. When we were in our teens in TLV, my sibs and I would go on late night hunts to find the best homemade malabi! Rose water is the ingredient that really sets it apart. I like to serve it in individual glass jars (Mason jars are a great option, but there are more decorative and inexpensive options online) and often send guests home with a couple of servings. Such a fun gift for bigger events like bridal showers or birthday parties.

PREP: **10 minutes**   COOK: **2 hours and 10 minutes** (including chill time)

3 cups **whole milk** or almond milk, divided

½ cup **cornstarch**

¼ cup **granulated sugar**

1 tablespoon **rose water**

⅓ cup **pistachios**, toasted and chopped, for garnish

Dried rose petals (see Note), for garnish

Special Equipment: 8× 4-ounce (236ml) glass jars with lids (such as Mason)

1. In a small bowl, pour 1 cup of the milk. Sprinkle in the cornstarch and whisk to dissolve. In a heavy-bottomed, medium saucepan, whisk the remaining 2 cups (480ml) milk with the sugar over medium heat until the sugar is dissolved. Whisk in the cornstarch mixture.

2. Whisking constantly, cook until the mixture comes to a simmer and thickens. Reduce the heat to medium-low. Switch to a wooden spoon or silicone spatula and stir until the mixture is popping with large bubbles. The whole process should take 5 to 8 minutes. Remove from the heat and stir in the rose water.

3. Pour the pudding into small glass jars with lids (such as 4-ounce [236ml] Mason jars) or dessert bowls, leaving at least ½-inch (12mm) space for the garnish. Refrigerate, uncovered, until completely cooled and set, about 2 hours. If storing for longer, put the lids on the jars, or cover the bowls at this point with plastic wrap, and refrigerate for up to 3 days.

4. Garnish each with a sprinkle of pistachios and dried roses. Serve chilled.

NOTE *Food-quality rose petals and buds are available at specialty food shops and Kalustyan's (foodofnations.com). Be sure to get edible rose products, and not ones that have been treated for potpourri.*

BERRY PAVLOVA
à la Jenna Lyons

Jenna wowed our group of girlfriends at my place out east when she whipped up this insane pavlova. It's literally the best one I've ever tried. This meringue-based dessert is overflowing with whipped cream and fresh fruit... (perfect for pranking), and she so generously spent time writing and shooting this recipe for you all to feature in this chapter. Allow plenty of time for the meringue shell to bake and then cool, as the cooling time helps crisp it. The idea here is to create a delicious, fun mess of crunchy, creamy, fruity deliciousness!

PREP: **30 minutes**   *COOK:* **6 hours and 30 minutes** (including resting and chill times)

FOR THE MERINGUE

5 large *egg whites* (see Note)

1½ cups *granulated sugar*

1½ teaspoon *cornstarch*

1 teaspoon *white wine*, cider, or distilled white vinegar

Pinch of *kosher salt*

½ teaspoon *vanilla extract*

FOR THE BERRIES

8 ounces (225g) *fresh strawberries*, hulled and sliced

6 ounces (170g) container *fresh blueberries*

6 ounces (170g) container *fresh raspberries*

1 tablespoon *light brown sugar*

1 teaspoon high-quality *balsamic vinegar*

FOR THE WHIPPED CREAM

2 cups *heavy cream*

2 tablespoons *powdered sugar*

1 teaspoon *vanilla extract*

Special Equipment: Stand mixer, hand-held electric mixer, or whisk

1. Preheat the oven to 350°F (180°C). Line a large baking sheet with parchment paper. Using an 8-inch (20cm) cake pan as a template, use a thick pen to draw a circle on the paper and turn it over so you can see it through the underside.

2. To make the meringue, place the egg whites in the bowl of an electric stand mixer. Place the bowl in a larger bowl of hot tap water and let stand, stirring occasionally, until the whites lose their chill, 3 to 5 minutes.

3. In the bowl of a food processor or the jar of a blender (in batches), process the sugar and cornstarch together until finely ground, about 1 minute.

4. Affix the bowl to the mixer stand and fit with the paddle attachment. Add the vinegar and salt. Beat on low speed until the whites form soft peaks. Increase the speed to medium-high. One tbsp at a time, add the superfine sugar mixture, and beat until the meringue forms stiff and shiny peaks. Beat in the vanilla. Using a silicone spatula, spread the meringue to fill the circle on the parchment, bringing up the sides to give it a bowl shape to hold the berries and cream later.

5. Place in the oven and immediately decrease the temperature to 300°F (150°C). Bake the meringue until it is pale beige, about 1½ hours. Turn off the oven and let the meringue cool completely in the oven, about 2 hours.

6. Meanwhile, for the berries, combine the strawberries, blueberries, and raspberries with the brown sugar and balsamic vinegar. Cover and refrigerate until chilled and juicy, about 3 hours.

7. For the whipped cream, in a chilled medium bowl, beat the cream, powdered sugar, and vanilla with a handheld electric mixer at high speed (or whisk) until stiff. (The cream can be refrigerated for up to 1 day. If it separates, whisk until thickened.)

8. To serve, carefully peel the meringue from the paper and place it on a platter. Fill the meringue with the whipped cream. Using a slotted spoon, add the berries, then drizzle all over with the berry juices. Cut and serve. Don't try to be neat—it won't happen!

NOTE *Eggs are easiest to separate when they are cold from the fridge. Save the yolks to use to make Flan (see page 211) or other recipes. But whites beat best when they are not cold, so warming them in a bowl of hot water before whipping is important for the best results. Or simply let the whites stand at room temperature for about 45 minutes before beating.*

BUTTER COOKIES
(Middle Eastern-style)

Here is another very easy recipe with a huge payoff. These melt-in-your-mouth cookies are usually decorated with a pistachio, but you can use a walnut half or a blanched almond. Allow time for the dough to chill before shaping. It's a recipe that kids love to make, as the shaping is easy and can be played around with. My dad literally did not start his day without a minimum of 6 cookies with coffee, and he loved when I brought him cookies. He used to say "cookies make me happy," and I think we all share that sentiment.

PREP: **50 minutes to 1 hour and 30 minutes (including chill time)** *COOK:* **12 to 15 minutes**

1 cup **unsalted butter**, at room temperature.

¾ cup (58g) **powdered sugar**

1 teaspoon **vanilla extract**

2 cups (280g) **all-purpose flour**

¼ teaspoon **kosher salt**

Whole pistachios, for decoration

Special Equipment: Hand-held electric mixer, Baking sheet, Parchment paper

1. In a large bowl, using an electric mixer on medium speed, beat the softened butter until creamy and smooth, about 1 minute. Gradually beat in the powdered sugar, and beat until the mixture is light and fluffy, about 2 minutes more. Beat in the vanilla extract.

2. In a separate bowl, sift the all-purpose flour and salt together. Using a wooden spoon, gradually stir the flour mixture into the butter mixture, and mix until a soft dough forms. Gather up the dough, wrap tightly in plastic wrap, and refrigerate until chilled and firm, 30 minutes to 1 hour.

3. Preheat the oven to 325°F (160°C). Line a baking sheet with parchment paper. Remove the dough from the refrigerator. Pinch off pieces and roll into 1-inch (2.5 cm) balls.

4. Flatten each ball slightly and press a pistachio in the center. Arrange the cookies on the prepared baking sheet, leaving a little space between each. They won't spread much.

5. Bake until the edges are just barely golden, but the cookies are still pale, 12 to 15 minutes.

6. Let the cookies cool a bit on the baking sheet and then move to a wire cooling rack. (The cookies can be stored in an airtight container at room temperature for up to 5 days.)

Mom's BAKLAVA

This is our family recipe for baklava, which may differ from others you've seen. My grandmother made baklava all throughout my childhood, and it's so much easier to prepare than it seems. We make it with sugar syrup, much lighter than the usual honey (which also works if it's all you have). I crush the nuts in a mortar with a pestle for a homey, rustic texture, but you can really use any method. I also prefer to cut my baklava into bite-sized shapes so that everyone can end the meal with a small, sweet treat. Your guests will enjoy indulging mindfully rather than feeling stuffed.

PREP: 1 hour and 25 minutes (including syrup chill time)
COOK: 3 hours and 45 minutes (including syrup soaking time)

1× 1-pound (454g) package of *frozen phyllo dough*, thawed (See Note)
1 cup *unsalted butter*, melted, plus extra for buttering the pan

FOR THE FILLING
1½ cups (195g) *walnuts*
1½ cups (195g) *raw, unsalted pistachios*
½ cup (100g) *granulated sugar*

FOR THE SYRUP
1½ cups (300g) *granulated sugar*
2 teaspoon *rose water*

Special Equipment: 9×13-inch (23x33cm) baking pan

1. To make the syrup, in a small saucepan, bring the sugar and 1 cup water to a boil over medium heat, stirring to dissolve the sugar. Remove from the heat, stir in the rose water, and refrigerate until chilled and thickened, at least 1 hour.

2. Preheat the oven to 350°F (180°C). Brush the inside of a 9×13-inch (23x33cm) baking pan with some of the melted butter.

3. To make the filling, in batches if necessary, crush the nuts in a mortar with a pestle until medium-fine. (Or chop the nuts with a large knife.) In a medium bowl, mix the nuts and sugar.

4. If necessary, cut the phyllo sheets to fit the baking dish. Layer 4 filo sheets in the bottom of the pan. Sprinkle about ¾ cup of the nut mixture over the filo. Repeat three times, and finish with 4 filo sheets.

5. Using a thin, very sharp knife, cut the pastry lengthwise into 4 strips, spaced equally apart and making sure to cut through all the layers to the bottom of the pan. Now make 6 diagonal cuts across the strips, equally spaced apart and being sure to cut to the bottom of the pan. You will have about 24 complete, and a few smaller, pieces. Dribble the melted butter evenly over the baklava, being sure it seeps through all layers.

6. Bake until the top is golden brown, 35 to 45 minutes. Remove from the oven and pour the syrup evenly over the top. Let stand to fully absorb the syrup, 2 to 3 hours. Following the markings, cut into diamonds and serve. (The baklava can be covered with plastic wrap and stored at room temperature for up to 2 days.)

NOTE *The secret to working with phyllo dough? Thaw it overnight in the refrigerator, never at room temperature. Slow, cold defrosting will keep the sheets from sticking together.*

Labneh CHEESECAKE
with Blueberry Topping

Cheesecake? I'm obsessed. It's a byproduct of growing up in NYC. I used to ask for cheesecake at all my birthday parties as a kid. But my other love is Middle Eastern and Mediterranean cooking. I've discovered the tangy magic that happens when you make a cheesecake with labneh. I also like my cheesecake with a light cookie crust instead of the graham-cracker kind, and a fruit topping, just like the very best bakeries on the Upper West Side used to make.

PREP: **30 minutes**   COOK: **6 hours (including cooling and chill time)**

Softened butter, for the pan

FOR THE CRUST
Unsalted butter (softened, for the pan)

1 cup *unbleached all-purpose flour*

¼ cup *confectioners' sugar*

½ cup *unsalted butter*, cut into ½-inch (12mm) pieces, at room temperature

1 teaspoon *vanilla extract*

FOR THE FILLING
2½ cups *thick Labneh* (see page 100) or use store-bought

1× 8-ounce (225g) package of *cream cheese*, softened

¾ cup *granulated sugar*

3 large *eggs*, at room temperature

2 teaspoons *vanilla extract*

Finely grated *zest of ½ lemon* (save fruit for topping)

1 tablespoon *cornstarch*

FOR THE BLUEBERRY TOPPING
2 cups fresh or frozen *blueberries*

¼ cup (50g) *granulated sugar*, or as needed

2 tablespoons freshly squeezed *lemon juice*

1 tablespoon *cornstarch*

Special Equipment: 9-inch (23cm) springform pan, Hand-held electric mixe, Roasting pan for water bath

1. Preheat the oven to 350°F (175°C). Lightly butter a 9-inch (23cm) springform pan. Tightly wrap a double thickness of aluminum foil around the bottom of the pan to waterproof it.

2. To make the crust, in a medium mixing bowl, whisk together the flour and powdered sugar. Add the butter and vanilla. Mix with an electric mixer at low speed until crumbly. Gather the dough together. Crumble the dough into the prepared pan and press firmly and evenly into the bottom and about ¼ inch (6mm) up the sides. Place the pan on a baking sheet. Bake the crust until set and starting to brown, about 10 minutes. Transfer the pan to a wire rack to cool while making the filling.

3. To make the filling, in a large mixing bowl, beat the labneh, cream cheese, and granulated sugar with a hand-held electric mixer on medium speed, scraping down the sides as needed, until smooth and creamy. One at a time, add the eggs, letting each be absorbed before adding another. Mix in the vanilla, lemon zest, and cornstarch until combined but not overmixed. Pour into the crust.

4. Put the springform pan in a larger roasting pan. Add enough hot tap water to the roasting pan to come halfway up the sides of the springform pan. Carefully transfer the setup to the oven. Bake until the cheesecake filling jiggles when shaken (the very center may look wet), 50 to 60 minutes. Turn off the oven and let the cheesecake cool in the oven with the door ajar for 1 hour.

5. Remove the cheesecake from the roasting pan and discard the foil. Cover loosely with plastic wrap and refrigerate until chilled and set, at least 4 hours or overnight.

6. Meanwhile, to make the topping, in a small saucepan over medium heat, combine the blueberries, sugar, and lemon juice. Cook, stirring occasionally, until the juices begin to thicken, about 10 minutes. In a small, glass measuring cup or bowl, pour 2 tablespoons water. Sprinkle in the cornstarch and stir to dissolve. Stir into the saucepan and cook, stirring often, until the mixture is boiling and thickened, about 2 minutes. Remove from the heat and cool completely.

7. Spread the blueberry topping evenly over the top of the cheesecake. Refrigerate until the topping is chilled and set, about 30 minutes. (The cheesecake can be refrigerated for up to 3 days.) Slice, dipping a thin knife into a tall glass of warm water between cuts, and serve chilled.

ALMOND AND OLIVE OIL CAKE
with Orange Glaze

Here's an easy citrusy cake for when you need something simple to serve with coffee or tea. It also makes a nice gift to bring to someone's house when you don't want to arrive empty handed. You're likely to have all of the ingredients on hand and it probably takes less time to make than going out the market to buy something.

PREP: **20 minutes**   *COOK:* **40 to 45 minutes (including cooling time)**   *TOTAL:* **About 1 hour**

FOR THE CAKE

1⅓ cups *almond flour*

1 cup *all-purpose flour*

1 teaspoon *baking powder*

½ teaspoon *baking soda*

1 teaspoon *kosher salt*

¾ cup *extra virgin olive oil*, plus more for the pan

¾ cup *granulated sugar*

2 large *eggs*, at room temperature

¾ teaspoon *vanilla extract*

½ teaspoon *almond extract*

Finely grated zest of 2 *oranges*

½ cup freshly squeezed *orange juice*

¼ cup *plain whole-fat yogurt* or sour cream

FOR THE GLAZE

1 cup *powdered sugar*

2 tablespoons fresh *orange juice*, plus more as needed

2 tablespoons *sliced almonds*, toasted, for decoration

Zest of 1 *orange*, removed with a vegetable peeler and cut into very thin strips (or removed in strips with a channel knife)

Special Equipment: 9-inch (23cm) round cake pan, parchment or waxed paper

1. Preheat the oven to 350°F (175°C). Oil and line the bottom of a 9-inch (23cm) round cake pan with a round of parchment or waxed paper.

2. In a medium mixing bowl, whisk together the almond flour, all-purpose flour, baking powder, baking soda, and salt. In a large mixing bowl, whisk the olive oil and granulated sugar until well combined. One at a time, whisk in the eggs, letting each be absorbed before adding the next. Whisk in the vanilla and almond extract, orange zest, and orange juice. Whisk in the yogurt. Don't worry if it looks curdled.

3. Using a silicone spatula, gradually add and fold in the flour mixture, just until combined. Do not overmix. Scrape the batter into the prepared pan and smooth the top.

4. Bake until a toothpick inserted into the center of the cake comes out clean, 30 to 35 minutes. Transfer to a wire cooling rack and let cool in the pan for 10 minutes. Run a knife around the inside of the pan to release the cake. Invert the cake onto the rack, remove the pan, and let cool completely.

5. In a small bowl, whisk together the powdered sugar and orange juice until smooth and about the consistency of thick, heavy cream, adding more juice as needed. Drizzle the glaze over the cooled cake. Sprinkle with the almonds and orange zest.

6. Let the glaze set. The cake can be covered with plastic wrap or stored in a large, covered container for up to 4 days. Cut into wedges and serve.

SERVES
8

Lemon-Lime
POPPY SEED CAKE

Jewish bakeries are known to use a generous amount of poppy seeds. My easy loaf cake gets a finishing soak to give a tart sweetness, extra moisture, and a glossy glaze, as well as browned butter for a richer flavor. Use large fruit to get the citrus juices needed for the glaze. My dad was a big fan of this one.

PREP: **35 minutes (including sugar infusion time)**
COOK: **About 1 hour (including cooling time)**
TOTAL: **1 hour and 35 minutes**

1 cup *granulated sugar*

Finely grated zest of 1 *lemon* (reserve fruit for juice)

Finely grated zest of 1 *lime* (reserve fruit for juice)

1¼ cups *all-purpose flour*

3 tablespoons *poppy seeds*

1¼ teaspoon *baking powder*

½ teaspoon *kosher salt*

6 tablespoons *unsalted butter*, plus more for the pan

3 large *eggs*, at room temperature

½ cup *powdered sugar*

½ cup *heavy cream*

3 tablespoons fresh *lemon juice*

3 tablespoons fresh *lime juice*

Special Equipment: 8½ × 4½-in (21.5 × 10cm) loaf pan, parchment or waxed paper

1. Preheat the oven to 350°F (180°C). Butter an 8½×4½-inch (21.5×10cm) loaf pan. Line the two long sides and bottom of the pan with a sheet of parchment or waxed paper like a sling, letting the excess paper hang over the sides.

2. In a medium bowl, using a handheld electric mixer, mix the granulated sugar and the lemon and lime zests to release the citrus oils. Set aside for 20 to 30 minutes to infuse. Whisk the flour, poppy seeds, baking powder, and salt in a medium bowl.

3. In a small saucepan over medium heat, melt the butter and bring to a boil. Boil until it stops sizzling and turns pale brown. Remove from the heat and cool slightly. Stir to mix in the browned specks on the bottom of the pan.

4. Add the eggs to the sugar and beat with the mixer on high speed until pale and thickened, about 3 minutes. Gradually beat in the cream. On low speed, add half of the flour and beat just until incorporated. Beat in half of the melted butter with its specks. Repeat with the remaining flour and butter. Scrape into the prepared pan.

5. Bake until golden brown and a toothpick inserted in the center of the cake comes out clean, about 50 minutes. Let cool on a wire cooling rack until warm, about 20 minutes. Use a skewer to poke holes in the top of the cake.

6. In a small bowl, whisk the powdered sugar, lemon juice, and lime juice to make a syrup. Pouring through a wire sieve, slowly drizzle the syrup evenly over the cake, stirring if needed to help it flow. Cool completely.

7. Pull up on the paper to unmold the cake and discard the paper. Slice and serve. (The cake can be wrapped in plastic wrap and stored at room temperature for up to 3 days.)

10-12

Chocolate Marble
BUNDT CAKE

Another one of my dad's faves (are you sensing a theme here?). Bundt cake is always a crowd-pleaser. Chocolate marble is simple, not too sweet, delicious, and always a hit. It's perfect from brunch to afternoon snacks to dinner parties and can be eaten with your hands or dressed up with whipped cream. Perfect when paired with coffee or tea!

PREP: 20 minutes   *COOK:* About 1 hour (including cooling time)   *TOTAL:* 1 hour and 20 minutes

2 cups **all-purpose flour**, plus more for the pan

1 cup **almond flour**

½ teaspoon **kosher salt**

¼ teaspoon **baking soda**

1 cup **unsalted butter**, at room temperature, plus more for the pan

3 cups **granulated sugar**

6 large **eggs**, at room temperature

1 teaspoon **vanilla extract**

½ teaspoon **almond extract**

1 cup **sour cream**

2 ounces (55g) **unsweetened chocolate**, melted and cooled (see Notes)

Powdered sugar, for garnish

Special Equipment: 10-inch (25cm) Bundt pan, Stand mixer

1. Preheat the oven to 350°F. Butter and flour a 10-inch (25cm) Bundt pan, preferably nonstick.

2. Whisk the flour, almond flour, salt, and baking soda in a medium bowl. In a stand mixer with the paddle attachment, beat the butter on medium speed until the butter is lighter, about 1 minute. Gradually beat in the granulated sugar and beat until the mixture is very fluffy and pale for 4 to 5 minutes. Don't skimp on the time. One at a time, beat in the eggs, letting each egg be absorbed before adding the next. Beat in the vanilla and almond extract.

3. Reduce the mixer speed to low. In thirds, add the flour mixture, alternating with two additions of the sour cream, scraping down the bowl often. Transfer about 2 cups of the batter to a medium bowl and mix in the melted chocolate. Spoon about half of the plain batter into the pan.

4. Add dollops of the chocolate batter. Top with the remaining plain batter. Run a dinner knife through the batters to swirl them, then smooth the top.

5. Bake until a wooden toothpick inserted in the center of the cake comes out clean, about 50 minutes (or about 10 minutes more if not using a nonstick pan).

6. Transfer to a wire cooling rack and cool for 20 minutes. Run a knife inside the pan's edge and tube to loosen the cake. Invert onto the rack and remove the pan. Cool completely. (The cake can be stored, wrapped tightly in plastic wrap or in an airtight container, for up to 5 days.) Just before serving, sift powdered sugar over the top. Slice and serve.

NOTES   *To melt the chocolate, put coarsely chopped chocolate in a small microwave-safe bowl. Microwave in 30-second intervals at medium power for about 2 minutes, or until almost completely melted. Remove from the oven, let stand for 2 minutes, and stir to melt completely, reheating if needed. Cool until tepid but still fluid.*

227
DESSERTS

SETTING THE STAGE

Entertaining has a lot in common with staging a home for sale. Both use artistry to create a unique, inviting environment. Here are the elements that get the party started even before your guests take a single bite of food.

FLOWERS

There are blooms for any color scheme, style, or tabletop, and they can be budget-friendly. I place small arrangements throughout the house, including bud vases in the bathrooms and small arrangements wherever there are snacks.

With table centerpieces, flowers should influence the forms and colors that you use everywhere else. No matter what, remember the cardinal rule: Never let a too-large centerpiece block the view or impede conversation across the table. For a simple look, I might place single pink lotus blooms in shallow bowls along the length of the table. Or use potted herbs or mini succulents from the supermarket's flower department. Herbs also make the table smell special for certain cuisines and events.

CANDLES

Candles are ideal decorations and mood setters that can provide a warm glow that lets you dim the overhead lights and turn off table lamps. Don't forget candles in the powder room. Let candles melt and drip into wild, eye-catching mini sculptures. But if you're using an heirloom tablecloth or a surface that is easily damaged, it's wiser to go with dripless candles or self-contained types like votives, pillars, or tea candles.

PLACE SETTINGS

I don't do stuffy dinner parties. Still, there's a basic logic to arranging a place setting. Forks to the left (salad fork on the outside), knives to the right, with the soup spoon to the top of the plate. I like to serve forks with dessert, unless I'm serving ice cream.

GLASSWARE

Don't obsess over the right glass for the right wine. One size fits all in my home unless it's a smaller, more curated meal. My personal fave, and for more casual evenings, I'll use short bistro glasses for wine, which I think is pretty chic, too. I am particular about using flutes instead of coupes for sparkling wines—it's not 1950. Be sure your glasses are spotlessly clean—dirty glasses drive me nuts!

TEXTILES

Let fabrics make your tabletop a stunning showpiece with exciting combinations of colors and patterns. Tablecloths are a formal look, and you don't have to use one, but some meals call for them (brunch). That being said, many tables feature a handsome surface that is better left uncovered. A runner is a good compromise.

PLACEMATS

Another way to soften the vibe of hard surfaces is with placemats. The same is true of napkins, which should look good but be absorbent and pleasant to touch. For an informal party, don't bother to iron them. Sometimes I love that crinkly linen look. Use napkin rings when it's appropriate (look for interesting ones on Etsy or Amazon) and skip fancy folding. That being said, I love a fancy fold for a big dinner party!

MENUS

Mezze Night

- The Best Damn Za'atar Meatballs with Tagliatelle (page 161)
- Iraqi Kibbeh (page 166)
- Israeli Salad (page 75)
- Hummus (page 99)
- Lachuch (page 83)
- Homemade Butter (page 103) & Homemade Mayo (page 93)
- Baklava (page 218)
- Pomegranate Cosmopolitan (page 197)

Cozy Shabbat Dinner

- Yemenite Soup (page 128)
- Kubaneh (page 59)
- Crispy Brussels Sprouts with Honey and Lime (page 96)
- Mahasha (page 129)
- Green Schug (page 104)
- Tahina (page 101)
- Labneh Cheesecake with Blueberry Glaze (page 220)
- Classic Paloma (page 185)

Weekend Brunch Feast

- Shakshuka (page 48)
- Greek Yogurt with Roasted Stone Fruit and Almonds (page 32)
- Jachnun (page 55) with Shabbat Eggs (page 44)
- Lachuch (page 83)
- Labneh (page 100)
- Hummus (page 99)
- Moroccan Cigars (page 80)
- Israeli Salad (page 75)
- Fried Eggplant (page 95)
- Banana Spinach Muffins (page 39)
- Lemon-Lime Poppy Seed Cake (page 225)
- Bloody Marias (page 194)
- Espresso Martini (page 186)

Light & Refreshing Breakfast Spread

- Grandma's Crustless Quiche (page 47)
- Greek Yogurt with Roasted Stone Fruit and Almonds (page 32)
- Banana Spinach Muffins (page 39)
- Immuno Mocktail (page 201)

Vegetarian Celebration

- Eggplant and Shiitake Parmesan (page 158)
- Kitchri (page 84)
- Lachuch with Tahina Sauce (page 83 and page 101) or Labneh (page 100)
- Almond and Olive Oil Cake (page 223)
- Mezcalita (page 189) and/or Immuno Mocktail (page 201)

Latin Flavor Fiesta

- Picadillo (page 137)
- Platanos (page 87)
- Tostones (page 88)
- Mom's Red Rice with Almonds and Raisins (page 149)
- Shredded Cabbage Salad (page 79)
- Abe's Favorite Cuban-Style Flan (page 211)
- Classic Paloma (page 185)

Rosh Hashanah Feast

- Spatchcocked Roasted Chicken with Israeli Spices (page 134)
- Mom's Basmati Rice with Dill and Lima Beans (page 150)
- Moroccan Cigars (page 80)
- Fried Eggplant (page 95)
- Tahina Sauce (page 101)
- Kubaneh (page 59) and butter
- Israeli Salad (page 75)
- Greek Salad (page 76)
- Baklava (page 218)
- Pomegranate Cosmopolitan (page 197)

Hanukkah Celebration

- The Best Chicken Schnitzel You'll Ever Have (page 152)
- Fried Eggplant (page 95) with Tahina Sauce (page 101)
- Zesty Roasted Potato Wedges (page 91) with Simple Homemade Ketchup (page 92)
- Lachuch (page 83)
- Chocolate Marble Bundt Cake (page 227)
- The Mexican 75 (page 198)

Thanksgiving Feast

- Thanksgiving Turkey T'bit (page 154)
- Mom's Basmati Rice with Dill and Lima Beans (page 150)
- Mom's Red Rice with Almonds and Raisins (page 149)
- Basmati Rice with Pine Nuts (page 151)
- Greek Salad (page 76)
- Shredded Cabbage Salad (page 79)
- Crispy Brussels Sprouts with Honey and Lime (page 96)
- From-Scratch Mac and Cheese with Broccoli (page 114)
- Taramasalata (page 72)
- Hummus (page 99)
- Labneh (page 100)
- Green Schug (page 104)
- Homemade Mayo (page 93)
- Tahina Sauce (page 101)
- Almond and Olive Oil Cake (page 223)
- Labneh Cheesecake with Blueberry Glaze (page 220)
- Pomegranate Cosmopolitan (page 197)
- Ultimate Dirty Martini with Blue Cheese Olives (page 193)
- Negroni (page 190)
- The Mexican 75 (page 198)

Christmas Eve Dinner

- Sambusak (page 122)
- Lamb and Beef Kofte (page 169)
- Labneh (page 100)
- Homemade Mayo (page 93)
- Linguine with Fresh Clams (page 118)
- Couscous with Vegetables (page 146)
- Butter Cookies (Middle Eastern-Style) (page 217)
- Classic Negroni (page 190)

New Year's Eve Feast

- Bourekas Braid (page 125)
- Moroccan Poached Salmon (page 157)
- Basmati Rice with Pine Nuts (page 151)
- Greek Salad (page 76)
- Dulce de Leche No-Churn Ice Cream (page 210)
- Espresso Martini (page 186)

Crowd-Pleasing Casual Dinner

- Spatchcocked Roasted Chicken with Israeli Spices (page 134)
- From-Scratch Mac and Cheese with Broccoli (page 114)
- Shredded Cabbage Salad (page 79)
- Chocolate Marble Bundt Cake (page 227)
- Lemon-Lime Poppy Seed Cake (page 225)
- The Mexican 75 (page 198)

Comforting Weekend Dinner

- Divorced Dad's Chicken in a Pot (page 133)
- Mom's Red Rice with Almonds and Raisins (page 149)
- Zesty Roasted Potato Wedges (page 91)
- Simple Homemade Ketchup (page 92)
- Ultimate Dirty Martini with Blue Cheese Olives (page 193)
- Abe's Favorite Cuban-Style Flan (page 211)

Ultimate Buffet

HOT MAINS
- The Best Chicken Schnitzel You'll Ever Have (page 152)
- Lamb and Beef Kofte (page 169)
- Iraqi Meat Dumplings in Beet Stew (Kubba Shwandar) (page 162)
- Moroccan Poached Salmon (page 157)

GRAINS & SIDES
- Couscous with Vegetables page 146)
- Mom's Red Rice with Almonds and Raisins (page 149)
- Basmati Rice with Pine Nuts (page 151)
- Zesty Roasted Potato Wedges (page 91)
- Greek Salad (page 76)
- Shredded Cabbage Salad (page 79)

BREADS & DIPS
- Bourekas Braid (page 125)
- Lachuch (page 83)
- Hummus (page 99) & Labneh (page 100)
- Green Schug (page 104)
- Simple Homemade Ketchup (page 92)

DESSERTS
- Baklava (page 218)
- Mini Malabis (page 212)
- Butter Cookies (Middle Eastern-Style) (page 217)

DRINKS
- Bloody Marias (page 194)
- Maximilian Affair (page 182)
- Classic Paloma (page 185)
- Espresso Martini (page 186)
- Immuno Mocktail (page 201)

ACKNOWLEDGMENTS

It feels surreal that I'm thanking anyone for anything in regards to a book! Thank you for allowing me to say, thank you. Sarah, thank you for believing in me from day one. Molly, you're a guiding light and such a special person to work with. Thank you for trusting my recipes and allowing my process. Thank you to the entire team behind the scenes. It was truly a blast to work with each and every one of you refining recipes with special thanks to Marah, and then running around the city to shoot at locations that mean so much to me. Thank you Jenna and Jake for taking the time to photograph your recipes with me. Thank you to my ENTIRE internal team! My Mezcalum girls, my managers, my assistant, I honestly could never have done this without your support.

To my family, thank you for showing up the way a family shows up! I'm so grateful to have you all in my life. To my mom and aunt who spent countless hours recalling my grandmother's recipes with me and even bringing her vintage china to the shoot so we could plate her food in the dishes. To my mother-in-law for giving me a step-by-step guide to her best Cuban recipes. To my husband and my kids who were so patient while we worked to get each perfect shot out east. Abe, I appreciate your support more than you know. You're always there to lift me up and your care is without consequence—it means the world to me and without you in the equation none of this makes sense.

Love you all. Now let's come together and eat!
Xo

INDEX

SOPHIE ELGORT

Native New Yorker, ERIN DANA LICHY, is currently one of the stars of the Bravo television series, *The Real Housewives of New York*. Erin holds a master of science degree in sustainable development from N.Y.U. A serial entrepreneur, Erin is the owner of an interior design-build firm whose work has been featured in *Architectural Digest, Elle Decor,* and *Vogue.* She is the co-founder of Mezcalum, an artisanal mezcal and the host of the *Come Together* podcast. Erin resides in New York City with her husband Abe and four children.